The Human Soul

The Human Soul

Karl König

Floris
Books

First published in 1959 in *The Cresset*
the journal of the Camphill Movement
First published by Floris Books in 1986
This second edition published in 2006
Second printing 2018

British Library CIP Data available
ISBN 978-086315-578-9
Printed in Great Britain by TJ International

Contents

Chapter 1. The Mind and the Unconscious 9

Modern psychology and the human soul 9
On mind and soul 11
Approaching the land of the soul 13
The mind, the soul and the unconscious 15
Laughing and weeping 18
Synopsis 22

Chapter 2. Eros and Psyche 25

The three regions of the soul 25
The intentional faculty of the soul 27
The transcendent nature of the soul 30
Desire and discrimination 33
Synopsis 36

Chapter 3. Pain and Anxiety 37

The landscape of the human soul 37
The problem of pain 40
The enigma of anxiety 46
Synopsis 51

Chapter 4. Fear, Shame and Anger 53

The language of the emotions 53
The meaning of anger 57
The phenomena of fear and shame 61
Three companions: fear, shame and anger 66
Synopsis 69

Chapter 5. Mood and Temperament   71

The human moods   71
Emotion, temperament and mood   74
The mechanism of different moods   79
The four temperaments   84
Mood and temperament in man and animal   89
Synopsis   91

Chapter 6. The Twelve Senses   93

The twelve senses of man   93
Sound, music and the intentional faculty of the soul   98
Light and the transcendent nature of the soul   103
Synopsis   107

Chapter 7. Consciousness   109

The problem of consciousness   109
The different forms of consciousness   113
'Awakeness' and the dimensions of consciousness   117
The evolution of consciousness and the unconscious   120
The nature of object-consciousness and the human soul   124
Synopsis   128

Chapter 8. Dreams   131

The land of dreams   131
The interpretation of dreams   134
The content of dreams   137
The dimensions of dreams   142
Various types of dreams   145
The nature of dreams   148
Synopsis   151

Bibliography   153
Index   157

This book was first published in 1959 as a series of articles in *The Cresset,* the journal of the Camphill Movement. Obviously many things have changed in psychology in the last half century, yet there is a continuing demand from readers anxious to learn from Karl Köning's approcah.

For this edition the language has not been changed: the book is offered as it was written at the time.

References are given by author, year of publication and page. Full title and publication details can be found in the bibliography. References to lectures by Rudolf Steiner include the date of the lecture in square brackets.

Floris Books
August 2006

Chapter 1

The Mind and the Unconscious

Modern pyschology and the human soul

It may seem somewhat frivolous to say that psychology does not deal with its own subject — the soul of man; yet it is true. Psychology deals on the one hand with the conscious mind of man, and on the other hand it tries to enter the vast realm of the unconscious. But the soul itself, this very being of man, is left out.

Is it possible to describe the difference between mind and soul, between the soul and the unconscious? Is it at all permitted to speak in scientific terms about the soul of man? Usually this word and the meaning behind it are used only by theologians and poets. Its value in the scientific language of today is almost nil; it is even less than nil, because those who use it are immediately suspected of being mystics or 'phoney' idealists.

Yet, when we try to understand the meaning of a term like 'in mind and soul', or any other expression in which the word 'soul' appears, we experience in this word something entirely different from what we mean with 'mind'. When the Gospel says: 'For what shall it profit a man, if he shall gain the whole world and lose his soul?' (Mark 8:36), the last word cannot be replaced by 'mind'. For it is with the help of the mind that we are able to gain the world, not with the soul. Are mind and soul polar opposites to one another? They are not; yet they are different, and this difference is not overcome by denying the reality of the soul and repudiating its existence.

This, however, is continually done today, and hardly any professional psychologist would even think of using the word 'soul', although he bears the name in his own title; for 'psychology' is the Greek word for 'knowledge of the soul'. McDougall (1923), for example, when trying to define the boundaries of psychology, is forced to evade the issue and says: 'The aim of psychology is to render our knowledge of human nature more exact and more systematic. …' He thus superimposes 'the aim' on the 'subject' and defines psychology as 'an understanding of human nature'. This, however, is also the object of anatomy, of physiology, of psychiatry, of anthropology and many other branches of natural philosophy and human science; they all contribute to our better knowledge of human nature.

Modern psychology, unable to recognize the human soul, but equally unable to deny its effects, substitutes other words for it. One such curtain veiling the image of the soul is the word 'personality'. There are 'personality-traits', 'personality-tests', 'personality-dimensions' and many more such mis-nomers; they hide the truth of the soul in order to ignore its existence.

The being of the soul is either denied or shamefacedly explained away. Drives and motivations, intelligence and atti-tudes, perception and factors exist. They are statistically mapped out and most often analysed and interpreted in a quite unbelievably stupid and childish way. 'Measure as many traits and motivations, reactions and factors as you can lay hands on; interpret in terms of animal behaviour, or substitute Freudian principles and all will be well.' This is one of the trends in modern psychology, influenced by semi-informed opinions in America and the sophisticated attitude of modern British phi-losophy.

And it is understandable when from among psychologists, a voice is suddenly heard saying: 'Psychology is the most undisci-plined of disciplines, the nursery and romping ground for every extravaganza, a Tower of Babel for every known and unknown tongue, a mint for counterfeit and spurious coins, a market place for every pedlar of far-fetched and unlikely theories' (Cohen 1958). If a professor of psychology speaks in such terms, we may believe him.

Psychology is a market place because it has denied the exis-tence of its own subject: the human soul. It is a Tower of Babel because more and more words, terms, names and categories are introduced to express what otherwise could simply be called — the human soul. It is a mint because instead of the reality, only its representation is dealt with in the form of coined abstractions.

Is it not better in this case to leave the boundaries of such modern psychological investigations behind us and dare to enter the unknown country of the human soul? Is it possible to grope one's way so far that a first dim light will appear?

On mind and soul

It would be futile to attempt to describe the meaning of the word 'soul'. It refers to something which we know exists some-where in the depths of our being, even if this existence is con-tinually denied or purposely veiled. To define the word 'soul' is as difficult as it is to define the word 'mind'. We already men-tioned the difference between these two entities, and we shall now try to ask our own inner understanding what we mean when we say 'mind' and what we feel when we speak about a 'soul'.

If we make language our teacher, we find a great variety of concepts covered by the word 'mind'. I can 'change my mind'; I may 'follow my mind'; I can 'make up my mind', and then decide to 'set my mind to something'. Each time the word 'mind' expresses the leading factor in my conscious life. This mind, which I follow, which I set to something, which suddenly discovers a thing and is changed by it, radiates like a light. Is it not a kind of lamp shining in an otherwise dark realm of myself?

There is, however, another meaning in this word. If I 'bear something in mind' or if I 'keep it in mind' or if I am 'in mind of something', it means that I remember, or even better, that I rec-ollect what otherwise would have disappeared into the vast unconscious realm of my memories. Here again 'mind' is meant to bring something to the light of consciousness and to save it from being forgotten.

The following sentences express yet another concept of the same word: when we say 'mind your own business', 'never mind him' or 'do you mind?' we appeal to the 'mind' of another person or of ourselves. What do I really want to say when I ask someone if he would 'mind' my doing a certain thing? I draw his attention to my intended work. In a similar way, I ask the other person not to give his attention to a special thing and therefore 'to mind his own business'. It is again the shining lamp which I address. 'Shine upon me', I say, 'and then tell me whether my deed can remain in your light.' Similarly, I beg another person to turn his light away and not disturb the glow of my own lamp.

If somebody is 'out of his mind', he has lost his better judgment. On the other hand, when several people are together 'of one mind', then their individual lights shine in unity without any discord.

However varied and manifold the meaning of this great little word may be, it always points to the light of consciousness. It describes that special part of our mental being which acts in the light of self-consciousness.

The origin of the word is a manifold one. It derives from the Anglo-Saxon *gemynd* which means 'memory'. It also has a root in the Anglo-Saxon *munan* which means 'to think', and it is deeply related to the Latin *mens*. The latter word is the same as 'mind'. It describes something like 'reason', 'intelligence', 'judgment' as in the Latin sayings *mens et ratio* and *mens sana in corpore sano*, meaning 'reason and ratio' and 'a sound mind in a sound body'.

Therefore we may connect 'mind' with *mens* and 'mental' as well as with *gemynd* and *munan*. They all, however, lead back to one single word and that is 'man'. Man is the being here on earth who is begotten with the light of consciousness: this is the mind.

Quite a different meaning lives behind the word 'soul'. Its sound alone is very different. The bright vowel in 'mind', which is similar to 'light', 'eye' and 'I' and 'high', to 'dry', 'mine' and 'thine', points out the shining clarity of our day-consciousness. 'Soul' however, has a dark sound as in 'hole' and 'hollow', but also in 'whole' and 'roam', in 'soar' and 'roar'. And soul and sound are close relatives.

This word is cognate with the Anglo-Saxon word *sawel* and the German *Seele*. It is not known where the root of these related words can be found. There are also very few sayings in the English language connected with the word 'soul'. We call somebody a 'good soul' or a 'poor soul', and neither expression is a very admiring one; both express rather a kind of benevolent superiority over the 'poor' or the 'good soul'.

On the other hand, there is the expression 'with heart and soul' and it means the innermost being of man. It is impossible to give more than 'heart and soul' to a task, because it contains everything a man can give. It is not the purposeful light of the mind, nor does it indicate the whole sphere of the consciousness. It means the 'whole and all', whatever a man has — his body and spirit, his heart and soul, he offers up to a certain thing.

Similarly when we are asked to confess 'on soul and conscience', we are not only meant to say the truth, but much more than the truth. We are meant to stand behind our statement with our entire existence.

The connection of the soul with the heart on the one hand, and the conscience on the other, is very indicative. It reveals the wisdom of language and points in the right direction.

We shall now take the light of our mind and try to enter the hidden land of our soul.

Approaching the land of the soul

In looking back into the land of that kind of 'human nature' which modern psychology has laid bare and open, we may ask ourselves: What is missing in all these drives, motivations, attitudes, traits and so on? The answer can soon be given. It is a grey and colourless country in which many things happen, but they happen without any kind of beauty; they have neither grace nor dignity — they simply are. And suddenly we realize that man as a person has been stripped of all his wonder and beauty, his pain and joy, in order to become an explicable existence.

'Stripped of his soul!' so stands man in the shameless neon-light of modern psychology. His face looks pale, more like a corpse than a living being.

And again we ask: What is this 'soul' that is missing here? When we try to look back in mind to our childhood and recollect some of our memories, every one of us will remember happy and unhappy experiences. There are scenes of our early days when we travelled with our parents, met our cousins, played with other children, and suffered defeat as well as glory. How colourful all these memories are! Each one of them bears some deep sentiments and many strong feelings, an armful of heart and courage.

I remember how once, being a child of perhaps seven or eight, I walked through a forest. It was a summer morning and I still see the sun shining through the thicket of the leaves. And suddenly I stopped, my heart began to race and a hitherto unknown terror gripped my being — in front of me appeared a snake; it lifted up its head and was looking at me. Nothing happened; my fear kept me motionless and the snake slithered away. I turned around and walked back to our home. My inner being was in uproar although I did not know why or how. At the same time I tried to comfort myself. From this moment on, I was different from what I had been before. Fear and the infinite, the unknown, were much nearer to me, and a certain amount of contemplation began to roam through my mind. The snake had awakened my life of thoughts.

Most of my early memories are full of colour and wonder; this is similar for most of us. Childhood had a colourful hue and a fairy-tale-like halo. The meanest thing was invested with magnificence and awe. Behind every door was a secret, behind every corner of the street a mystery. The figures of our fantasy were much more real than the living ones around us. How strange and foreign could the parents be when we toiled and suffered with Robinson Crusoe, when Gulliver led us into the land of dwarfs and giants and we probably experienced his adventures in a much stronger and more lively way than he himself. At such times, our parents were almost shadows, and school a land of hazy existence, shrouded in mist and unreality.

Were not the first friendships overpowering in their experience? How deeply I adored my first friends! How I loved and admired the first little girl who made an impression on me!

Who was this 'me'? It was the same as I am now, and yet how different! With heart and soul were we engrossed in all our experiences; every event was an adventure and every meeting an unforgettable occasion. We minded the evening for it made the day cease!

On other occasions, we wished that no more days would come, because our conscience was burdened with guilt and we could hardly imagine how to continue living. Our sentiments were strong and colourful; they filled the cup of our existence right up to the brim, and images, fantasies, dreams soared up and down.

We ran through the streets, unprotected by anything and unaware of all the dangers which roamed about. A veil of safety surrounded our doings and our bodies functioned without any apparent conscious guidance. As if on a tightrope, with eyes blindfolded, we walked through life until step by step, and by and by, the mind began to take form. Its light began to radiate; we started to set our mind to certain tasks. We kept our lessons in mind, we minded our environment, we followed the teacher's mind, and called to mind the school subjects.

The brighter the lamp of the mind became, the more the colours of the soul faded away. The reality of the outer world assumed more and more importance, and a cloud started to shroud our inner experiences. Our fantasies became less vivid and our sentiments less apparent. Just as the growing light of the sun extinguishes the sparkling starry sky at dawn, so does our mind in the course of childhood and youth obliterate the colourful life of the soul. But the stars, although they disappear during the light of the day, still follow along their courses. In a similar way do the faculties of the soul continue to live and to work behind the sun of our mind. To get to know ourselves means to learn to discover again the starry realm of our soul.

The mind, the soul and the unconscious

The differentiation between 'mind' and 'soul' is a preliminary step towards a first understanding of the human being. It is interesting that the German and the Scandinavian languages have no word that compares to the meaning of 'mind'. It is extremely difficult to find a correct German translation for it; in each single instance it would have to be replaced by an approximate expression.

'Mind' stems from the Latin 'mens'. And it was in Rome and later in the Latin countries that the light of the mind unfolded in the course of history during the last three millennia. From Gaul and Rome, the growing mind penetrated into the Anglo-Saxon world and transformed its ethnological background. In the Teutonic countries 'mind' did not shine as brightly as it did in the Latin ones. But here the nightly being of the soul was still prevalent and the sun of the mind was only like a morning dawn. It is now different, but it is still not possible to give 'mind' a proper name. In the northern parts of the European continent, the mind is not so detached from the soul as it is in Britain, and this is the reason for its not being called and named by a separate word.

In the same way that the mind develops out of the soul's existence during childhood and youth, another part of our being retreats into the realm of the unconscious. Just as the full moon descends in the western sky when the sun is rising, so do our motives and intentions sink into the night of the unconscious when our mind is being formed. What lies bare and open during childhood disappears at puberty into the hidden folds of the soul's night. The sun of the mind rises and the moon of our volition descends. Our drives, instincts and motivations recede into the unknown realms of the unconscious. Psycho-analysts try to 'gate-crash' into this hidden land and in doing so may inflict untold damage on thousands of people. What is today described as psycho-analytical treatment is often a form of slight depersonalisation of the patient. It is often very difficult for a person to recover from this insult. The realm of the night cannot be entered into with the electric bulb of the modern intellect. For this a quite different approach is needed.

We now realize that there are two spheres within ourselves, the mind and the unconscious. They are opposites, and are somewhat comparable to our experience of external day and night. There is, however, one big difference. Within ourselves, day and night do not alternate, but both are continually present. When we are awake, our mind shines and our unconscious is darkened; in sleep this is different. In a later chapter we shall try to describe this special condition of human existence.

It will be helpful in our understanding of mind, soul, and unconscious to consider the two human attributes, dignity and grace. We can say that dignity is an attribute of the mind, while grace is an attribute of the unconscious. Dignity is the highest expression of the mind. In dignity, the rays of the mind are gathered around a self-conscious personality who is able to control his motives. The mind has gained the ability to rule over the drives and to know the motives of its actions. A kind of crown of consciousness surrounds the mind in dignity.

On the other hand, grace is the fulfilment of all our motives that live in the unconscious. In grace, they no longer serve a purpose and try to achieve it in the best possible way; they willingly submit themselves to a higher order and become selfless. They assume a condition of self-surrender and reveal not their own, but a divine law. An Indian temple-dance, or a piece of curythmy perfectly executed, unfolds the secret of grace.

Both, however, dignity as well as grace, live not in a sort of splendid isolation, but belong to the human soul. They are part of it and the soul provides them with certain attributes. The garment of grace is a serene and happy disposition; that of dignity, a serious and earnest attitude. These sentiments invest the two dignitaries of the soul with colour and substance. Grace will always be enveloped in a cloak of ease and happiness, and dignity enwrapped in a somewhat stern seriousness. An earnest kind of grace would be as unnatural as a joyful dignity. When they appear like this, it always has a fanciful and artificial touch.

The human soul endows grace and dignity with these garments, making them human and acceptable. The soul surrounds the sphere of the unconscious with a mantle of joy and gladness, and it envelops the mind with a cloak of earnestness and gravity.

The sentiments of the human soul are similar to the colours in nature. The bright and lovely colours of happiness are laid around the night-existence of the unconscious; the stern and dark colours of the serious attitude accompany the light of our mind.

In children we can very often observe how in the morning when the sun of the conscious mind breaks through the mist of dreams, the mood is earnest and restrained. In the evening on the other hand, when bedtime comes, the mood suddenly swings into unbounded gaiety when everything is fun and laughter. The joy and happiness of the unconscious draw near in the evening.

It is, therefore, not surprising that men like Freud and Bergson, who as psychologists explored the realm of the unconscious, met the problem of laughter, wit and humour at the borderland of their field of research.

Recognizing all these phenomena, we already find ourselves within the precincts of the human soul. The sentiments are like colours and indicate a twofold nature in their swing between joy and sorrow. The brightly coloured joy of carmine-red changes through many different shades into the dark blue of deep sorrow. If either of the bright or dark colours reaches such a degree of tension in the soul that it is too much for us to bear, we either burst into tears or into laughter. There is no better word than 'burst' to describe this process; it is a spilling over of joy or sorrow.

Laughing and weeping

Among the most striking characteristics of man are his emotional outbursts of weeping and laughing. They are common to almost every human being; they belong to all races and are the ever-present companions of humanity.

A good amount has been written on laughing, much less on weeping, and a very small amount of knowledge and understanding is available for such common expressions of human nature. In one of the best books dealing with these two phenomena, Professor Plessner wrote (1950): 'Laughing and weeping are two forms of expression which, in the true sense of the word, are available only to man.' This is a fundamental fact; no animal can weep or laugh. It may be able to shed tears, to cry, to grin, sometimes even to have a faint smile in its eyes, but to laugh heartily or to weep bitterly is given only to man.

But Plessner, pursuing his statement, at once has to add that though these two forms of expression are so singularly human, they show man in a rather unhuman position. 'The one who laughs or weeps loses in a certain sense his control over himself and thus the possibility to form an objective opinion on the situation he is in.' This again is a fundamental thought. Man is overcome by laughing as well as by weeping. He is usually quite unable to suppress these two emotions; he can hide them behind a smile, a stern look or behind a handkerchief, but the emotions themselves run their course.

Laughing and weeping are by far stronger than other human expressions. We can much more easily refrain from speaking; we can also suppress our gestures if we do not want to make use of them, but to escape from a burst of laughter is as difficult as it is to overcome the first sobs in weeping. It is as if an unknown power would force itself upon us and keep us in its grip. Who among us has not experienced the strength with which laughter encroaches upon us in moments when we want to be particularly serious? But perhaps a thought, a memory, or a funny situation which only we discover, forces us to a sudden burst of repeated laughter.

It is very surprising that most of the authors who write about laughing are much more concerned with its cause than with laughter itself. They inquire into the nature of the ludicrous, of wit and fun and comedy. The event itself, how laughter occurs, is usually overlooked. For this reason, several writers on this subject ask the question as to whether laughing and weeping are related at all. Some of them think that the two have actually no connection but have two different origins. We shall not mention here all the ideas and explanations which try to expound upon the nature of weeping and laughing.

Rudolf Steiner gave several lectures on weeping and laughing and showed the intimate connection of these two expressions to the function of breathing. He pointed out that in weeping as well as in laughing, the rhythms of inhaling and exhaling are altered. Instead of the regular intake and output of air, in weeping several short inhalings are followed by a long and deep exhaling. The opposite happens in laughing; there is a staccato exhaling followed by an extensive and long-drawn-out inhaling. These patterns of breathing are repeatedly enacted and present, as it were, the physical foundation of laughing and weeping.

These two patterns are exactly reciprocal to each other and it often happens that laughter can change into weeping, and weeping into laughter. These phenomena show strikingly the deep relationship of the two expressions. Laughing and weeping are non-identical twins in the life of the human soul.

Are we able to explain these patterns of changed breathing? What does it mean that in weeping the act of *inhaling* is broken up into several small bits and is then followed by a deep sigh of relief? We succumb to weeping when something in our surroundings assumes such an overpowering might that we are unable to bear it. When the loss of someone we loved is realized, but also when a friend or relative whom we had missed for months or years, comes back to us, we burst into tears. It is the new situation which has forced itself on us and become so strong and overwhelming that we can only meet it in small fractions. Therefore we inhale the surrounding air in small bits and after having done so, we are relieved and release a sigh of deep satisfaction; we exhale in a prolonged breath.

In a similar way, laughing occurs when something ludicrous happens. But what is — or appears to be — ludicrous to us? We love to see a comedy because it gives us the satisfaction that we are more reasonable and clever than those on the stage. 'How stupid, how ridiculous these people are! These clowns of life, these drunkards and funny persons!' This is our reaction and we feel stronger and bigger than they. When we look at a caricature, we are relieved that strong Khrushchev or Stalin or the domineering person of de Gaulle suddenly turn into comical figures. Their strength is at least for the moment diminished; we are relieved and start to laugh. As we feel stronger than that which is around us, we burst into repeated bits of exhaling and thus unload our strength into the world after which, being slightly exhausted, we inhale deeply in order to balance our loss.

A disturbance in our relationship to the world is the cause for weeping and laughing. When the world is too strong and seems to overwhelm us, weeping sets in; when on the other hand, the world is weak, small and tiny, a burst of laughter is the result. Both weeping and laughing are given to us in order that we may again balance the lost equilibrium for our contact-situation. They are like remedies; they restore a condition which has lost its proportions.

It would be wrong to imagine that laughing is an expression of joy, and weeping one of sorrow. They do not express an emotion, but they are an emotional act which in turn heals an emotional sickness. The basic principle of homoeopathy, *similia similibus curantur* (a substance can create the disease as well as heal it), is applicable in weeping and laughing.

And something more has to be understood; even Plato (in *Philebus*) when speaking about the nature of laughter, points out that both pleasure and pain are contained in it. And we can add that pleasure is embodied in the staccatos of exhaling. The deep inhaling, however, which follows like the answer to a question, carries in it a certain amount of shame and pain. A feeling of guilt lives in us after a bout of laughter, and here lies the root of the double nature of every comedian; outwardly he jokes, but inwardly he is often filled with sorrow.

Equally, weeping is not just pain and grief; only the short and repeated gasps of inhaling are the sad side of it. The deep exhaling brings relief and pleasure and restores the lost equanimity. It answers the question of grief.

Plessner is quite justified to call weeping and laughing borderline reactions. 'We weep and laugh,' he says, 'in a situation for which we find no other answer.' Instead of a rational answer, the reactions of weeping and laughing occur. But it is not a bodily, it is an emotional answer. We are shaken and jolted in full measure and there is no escape from it until a certain degree of restitution is reached.

Weeping and laughing in their highest sense are nothing less than a catharsis through which we pass. It is the same catharsis of which Aristotle speaks when he describes the influence of drama on the human soul.

Weeping and laughing are guardians who stand at two different gates; laughing guards the gate of the unconscious, weeping keeps the door of the mind. When our unconscious suddenly bursts through its gate because we are tempted by the ludicrous to throw ourselves too far out into the world, the guardian of laughter appears and restores our equilibrium. On the other hand, when our mind is overwhelmed with awe and unbalance so that we lose our sense of proportion, weeping steps forward and offers its comforting touch.

It is the soul that through the powers of laughter and weeping restores the mind as well as the unconscious to their own realms and rights. The soul's laughter sends our megalomania back into the sphere of the unconscious; the soul's weeping removes the inferiority feeling of our mind and leads it back to its place of habitation.

Synopsis

Many a fairy tale speaks about giants and dwarfs. And many people are convinced that such beings never existed. Yet they not only existed once upon a time, but they are still with us. They exist within us, imprisoned in our own being, serving, helping and often also overpowering and ruling us.

Our unconscious is the giant in us. He is imprisoned like the genie in the flask who continually tries to escape. Laughter is set as his guardian and helps to keep him at bay.

Our mind is the dwarf in us; small and witty, clever and cruel, as he appears in the fairy tale. Tom Thumb is the mind and when he loses his way in the thicket of the worldly forest, the maiden weeping appears and shows him the way back to his home.

When the giant of our unconscious is not only tamed but transformed and moulded, then grace begins to appear. When the dwarf of the mind grows up, matures and becomes human, dignity unfolds.

Images now appear; the soul begins to speak of itself, to name itself and to describe its being. The following drawing is an attempt to bring together the first phenomena we have described.

Chapter 2

Eros and Psyche

The three regions of the soul

Heraclitus, the Greek philosopher and teacher at the temple of Ephesus, described the human soul by saying: 'You will never be able to fathom her boundaries, even when you tread all existing roads, so extensive is her being.'

And Zeylmans in the opening chapter of his book (1953) on the human soul writes:

> This mysterious being we call 'soul' has the most varied and opposite faculties. It is at the same time omnipresent and hardly discernible; it is widely open and narrowly closed; it is mighty as well as tender. Ideas of the infinite and transitory desires lodge there close to one another. When we make an attempt to get to know the soul, we must not shrink from accepting it with all its contradictions. We may even discover that just the fact that the soul possesses such paradoxical qualities is one of its most important characteristics.

These two statements, the one of an ancient, the other of a modern philosopher, both of great distinction, give a most comprehensive indication of the complexity and vastness of our subject. It will take us far and wide into the fields of human nature, and we shall never be satisfied with our results in trying to understand the human soul. We shall always have to begin anew and find other approaches and fresh paths.

In our first attempt, we laid out the various realms of the human soul. We distinguished an upper sphere where the mind is concentrated, and an opposite part which harbours the unconscious. The realm between these two is a connecting link where weeping and laughing live.

Thus a kind of sketch of the geography of the soul was drawn up to give us the possibility of gaining a first orientation of the regions in which we have our mental existence. In the upper pole where the mind works, is the sphere of our thoughts. Here we also are conscious of our daily doings; we accompany our actions with sense and reason; we create our concepts of the world around us. This is the region of the observing dwarf.

In the lower pole where our unconscious is housed, lives our will. From here we realize our intentions, desires, longings and wishes. It is the region whence our drives and motives arise. Our anger and our passion to rule emanate out of this realm. It is the sphere of the sleeping giant who time and again wakes up and overpowers our conscious being.

Between these two poles lies the third realm whence our feelings have their origin. This is the part in which the soul reveals itself in its most genuine form. All our experiences, our deeds and our thoughts are accompanied by sentiments. There is not a single observation, not the smallest intention without some touch of feeling. The things we see, the sounds we hear, the work we perform are coloured by our feelings. It is the very nature of our feelings that they form the undercurrent of all our experiences. Our daily life is not only filled with emotions, but it proceeds alongside our feelings and sentiments. These carry our mental existence as a river carries its ships. We may even say that the very essence of the soul is revealed in the life of our feelings.

A subtle self-observation discovers some qualities of the sentiments. We can experience them as being of an exceedingly transient nature. As soon as we try to take hold of them, they vanish away. I can drive my joy away when I grow too conscious of it; and my sorrow disappears when I try to look it in the face. The light of our mind can dispel the tender waves of our feeling-life.

This emotional undercurrent is really like a river; its waves constantly come but never stand still or remain. A continuous flow carries them off again. We experience this current as our feelings; our subconscious knowledge of the flux of time is ultimately related to the river of our emotions.

The character of our feelings is twofold; they can like or dislike. Their attitude is either a sympathetic or an antipathetic one. Whatever we meet or do or experience comes under this influence. A person whom we meet, a job we carry out, the appearance of a thing — is either liked or disliked. This twofold possibility need not be very outspoken and obvious, but in some way it is always there. When it is enhanced, it rises to love or hate. These two emotions are the strongest exponents of our life of feelings.

When we like and love, we extend the being of our soul and try to embrace our experiences with its substance. The opposite happens when we hate or dislike. Here the soul undergoes a process of contraction and shrinks away from the world. Our feeling-life is like the beat of the heart. It consists of expanding and contracting attitudes like the systole and diastole of the heart's activity. It is however arhythmical, mostly selfish, self-concerned and personal. Yet it carries our daily experiences and runs very forcibly through our dreams.

With this description of the middle region of the soul, we have gained a further insight into its geographical layout. We begin to distinguish the three districts and can envisage them as the land of the mind where the light of the consciousness shines. Between the light and the darkness, the constantly changing colours of feelings occur. They give the lively and beautiful background to our mental existence.

The intentional faculty of the soul

One of the greatest sages of our time, Edouard Schuré, called the human soul *la clef de l'univers* — the key of the universe. It is not difficult to understand this sentence when we try to make some special observations about the very being of the soul. One of the most important characteristics belonging to our mental experiences is their intentional quality. What does this mean? The first modern philosopher and psychiatrist to describe this condition was Franz Brentano. In several of his books he tried to develop a better understanding of the intentional activity of the soul.* Other philosophers like Husserl and Scheler continued to investigate this subject, and Rudolf Steiner referred to it extensively ([1917] 1970, 1983).

When Brentano described it, he said (1889):

> The common characteristic of psychic activity consists in an intentional relation to something which perhaps is not real, but has nevertheless an inner objectivity. No hearing without something heard, no faith without something that can be believed, no hope without something to hope for, no aim without a goal, no joy without something that gives pleasure, and so on.

The whole life of our soul has this intentional character. Our emotions, our thoughts, our volitions are hardly ever without an object. We think and feel and will things, beings, deeds, experiences, anything outside ourselves. This is a simple truth but an important one. Our soul is constantly concerned with its surroundings and kept astir by the change of the experiences it can make.

Our sense-perceptions as well as the more subtle influences of our environment such as weather, temperature, the condition of our bodily organs and tissues, all provide the soul with experiences and facts to which an intentional connection is developed. Our thinking needs a content for its activity. Our feelings have an object for their actions. Our willing fulfils an intention to achieve its purpose.

All three — thinking, feeling and willing — are intentional in character. Their relation to the objects, however, is different in each of these three spheres of mental life. In the realm of thinking, we leave the object as it is, but have the urge to understand and to describe it. In the realm of feeling, we long for the object or try to avoid it. In the realm of willing, we want

---

* Even Plato and Aristole mention the intentional activity as a fundamental characteristic of mental processes.

to possess the object and, having achieved this, to give it away again.

The fundamental activity of intentionality is present in all three spheres, but is differentiated in a threefold way. Our thoughts have no possessive attitude; they keep at a distance to the object and it remains a kind of image, a mere semblance. Rudolf Steiner once described this fact in the following words ([1924] 1983, 22): 'The human soul exists, but Nature can only approach this human soul by becoming mere semblance.'

In the realm of feeling, the soul has a closer relation to the objects. It desires or avoids them and we experience this attitude as like or dislike and call it sympathy and antipathy. The screen of imagery which exists in the realm of our thoughts falls away and a first contact with the reality starts. The objects somehow begin to belong to us.

In the sphere of our will, we make the closest possible acquaintance with reality. Our hands take hold of it and use or misuse it. Every creative process in whatever realm it occurs is an act of possession in the sphere of the will. Whether I write or paint, plough or build, speak or model — the object undergoes an act of submission to my will. The final result is usually a distinctive feeling of humiliation which remains in the soul. The fulfilled deed leaves an experience of tiredness and shame behind. Rudolf Steiner described this with another sentence: 'Nature exists, but man can only approach her by letting her destroy him.'

The complete union between the soul and the object which has submitted itself creates the temporary extinction of the human being in the sphere of will. The experience of humiliation is the result. The conqueror turns into the conquered.

It is now justified to speak of three different forms of intentional acts: one which takes place in the sphere of the mind, the next which occurs in the realm of our emotional life, and the third in the region of the unconscious. Metaphorically speaking, we can liken the soul to the water of a river. On its surface it mirrors the colours of the sky and the objects on the banks. Its waves play an intimate game of give-and-take with the surrounding air and light. Down in the water, the teeming life of fish and many other creatures goes on. This is the intentional setting of a stream. And we can understand how Goethe, when he saw the majestic waterfall at Schaffhausen, wrote a poem the opening verses of which say:

> The human soul
> Is like the water;
> From heaven it comes,
> To heaven it rises,
> And down again
> To earth it descends,
> Eternally changing.

In these sentences a first understanding arises for the word of Schuré, *L'âme est la clef de l'univers*.

The transcendent nature of the soul

Besides the intentional quality, the soul has another fundamental characteristic. This is generally described as its transcendent nature. It is the faculty 'of becoming aware of the surrounding world which does not belong to ourselves but represents another entity' (Lersch 1943). A clear distinction is to be made between the intentional and the transcendent qualities of the soul. The first describes the ability of the soul to contact the surrounding world; the second, the faculty of becoming aware of this contact. The latter is a more inward quality than the former and is of special significance for a further understanding of the nature of the soul.

An unbiased self-observation which tries to watch the passing of mental experiences, very soon faces the following problem: How does it come about that I not only have the faculty of observing events outside myself, but also of reproducing them in the form of ideas and images? How is it possible that a flower I have just seen, a melody I have just heard, an event I have just experienced does not only remain an outward thing, but becomes part of myself?

To say that this is due to our power of memory is only to shift the problem to a different level, without solving it. Apart from the fact that memory is altogether another faculty which comes into action when inner concepts are already achieved, we must ask what it means that we are able to reproduce the facts and things of our surrounding world. Memory is the power which can retain these reproductions for longer or shorter periods. There cannot be any doubt that mental life possesses this ability.

It is the folly of modern psychologists to overlook this fundamental problem and to replace it by the nonsensical postulation that our sensory organs are the place where these reproductions are made. If that were so, how could we ever become aware of all we see and hear and touch and taste? The physical organs of sense are necessary for the act of perception. Yet they are only mediators between the soul and the world, whereas the soul itself has the function of creating an image of outer events and of retaining this image, even of recreating it at will and at leisure.

When we earnestly consider this statement which is based on simple daily experience, we must inquire as to the seat or place of this reproducing faculty. Where do we experience the flower we have just seen when we close our eyes and try to imagine it again? Where do we hear the melody which has just faded away while we are still able to reproduce it? Is there a space in which these ideas and concepts live? Or do they just occur 'within ourselves'?

It would be equally wrong to state that our thoughts live in our head. They are certainly connected to the head, but are not inside it. The same is true of our feelings and emotions. When we ask a child where he 'feels' love or anger, he will point to his heart. Our emotions are related to the heart, but they are as little inside the heart as the thoughts are inside the brain.

Such considerations give a first idea of the complexity of the problem we encounter. They also give a first understanding for the fact that the soul is a reality beyond our immediate grasp. The philosophers who speak about the transcendent quality of the soul simply describe the fact that this soul is able to take hold of things outside itself, and in reproducing their appearances, to retain them. (With 'appearance' I do not only mean their shape and colour, but also their possible smell, sound, touch, taste, mobility, and so on). Is it a photographic activity that here reveals itself? This is hardly the case, because these inner reproductions differ considerably from the outer things they copy. We can only describe this faculty as a creative one. The soul continually recreates the outside world in images and our sensory organs provide the substance by which these pictures are produced. Thus the created concepts and ideas are of a transient character; as soon as they appear, they dissolve again and a certain effort is needed to retain them for even a short while.

Here we again meet with the ever-flowing nature of the soul. It is never at rest, never finished, never fixed. It comes and, as soon as it is recognized, it disappears again. Becoming and going are the innate qualities of the life of the soul and our being is destined by them. Birth and death are but magnified occurrences of what otherwise constantly happens in the realm of the soul.

The being of our mental condition is transcendent. This transcendent being has the ability at the same time to take hold of and to recreate its surroundings as well as to be aware of both the surrounding world and its created image. These transcendent acts depend on the physical organs of the senses, but are not enacted by them. The senses are merely instruments and material for the transcendent activity of the soul, just as colours, brushes and canvas are needed by the artist to make his images appear.

This transcendent faculty cannot be found in the special world of our body; it is beyond it. It is nevertheless real and not an illusion. We rely on our images, ideas and feelings as much as we trust in the percepts of the outer world. We ascribe a different reality-value to the world outside by calling it 'permanent'; our mental life we regard as 'transient'. However, this transient being of the soul enables us to realize and become aware of the permanent existence of the outer world.

If this world were transcendent like our soul, it would appear to be as transient as our mental processes. The transcendent, transitory nature of the soul makes it the key of the universe. It has the ability to imagine, to reproduce, to recreate all the things that exist in the world. From the stars in heaven to the stones on earth, from the cry of an animal to the subtle melody of a harp — all is mirrored and known in the realm of the soul.

Desire and discrimination

The intentional and transcendent qualities are two fundamental characteristics of our mental life. We have tried to describe them and are now confronted with the problem of fitting them into the pattern of the soul. Where do these qualities originate? Have they their seat in the soul or do they only pass through it? Does the soul consist of intentional and transcendent qualities or are there other faculties of equal importance? How are the mental acts such as feeling, willing and reasoning related to them?

In several of his lectures on psychology. Rudolf Steiner describes a twofold nature of the soul ([1910 Nov 1] 1980, 1971). On the one hand, he points to the mental activity of discrimination (*Urteilen*), and on the other hand, to the twin activities of love and hate. He says: 'Discrimination* is the one activity of our soul. The sum total of all the other acts exhausts itself in the inner experiences that can be described as love and hate. These two activities encompass the whole life of the soul.'

He then continues to characterize these two mental processes and comes to the following conclusion: 'Behind the activity which appears as love and hate in us, desire [*Begehren*] always stands, irradiating the soul. On the one side, desire flows into the life of the soul and appears as love and hate. On the other side, the act of discrimination leads to the formation of concepts.'

Thus, discrimination is a mental activity which continually creates concepts and images. By means of this activity, we are

---

* I venture to translate the German word *urteilen* with the English word 'discrimination'. This rendering is by no means a correct one, but probably the nearest to the psychological meaning of *urteilen*. It is not 'judging' or 'judgment' in the usual sense of the word. Rudolf Steiner uses it in the way Franz Brentano used it. To him *urteilen* is a mental act by which we are able to assert the reality of our images and percepts. We 'discriminate' as to their nature.

able to form an adequate mental picture of the world around us. As soon as we understand this, we meet in the discriminating faculty an activity similar to the one we described as the transcendent quality of the soul. Its creative possibilities and image-forming power are contained in the process of discrimination.

Desire, however, rising up from the depths of the unconscious and revealing itself as love and hate, like and dislike, sympathy and antipathy, is deeply related to the intentional quality. What else can it be but desire that binds the soul to the surrounding worlds and fastens it to their things and beings? We can almost say that the core of the intentional process is desire. This quality of longing, of striving for everything which is not the soul but its surrounding lies at the bottom of intentionality.

The discriminating activity, on the other hand, contains transcendent qualities; the latter give to the reasoning soul the power of the continuous creation of concepts and images. It is a process which remains within the boundaries of the soul itself, because the transcendent abilities have made the surrounding world into a part of the soul. The transcendent quality conveys to the soul the material for its discriminating activity, whereas the radiating strength of desire connects the soul to its surroundings and thus creates its intentional quality.

Now we are able to relate all this to the 'geography' of the soul. It becomes obvious that the process of discrimination is the fundamental force behind the mind. Our concepts, ideas and images are contained in this realm; there they have their field of appearance. Concepts rise and fade away again in the light of the conscious mind. The power of thinking lives in this region and from the moment we wake up to the moment we fall asleep, this mind is the centre of our daily mental life. Behind it stands the creative activity of the transcendent power of the soul which reveals itself in the process of discrimination.

The other activity of the soul is desire. It arises from the unconscious region and irradiates the continuous stream of intentional acts. They reveal themselves in the sphere of our emotions and feelings; here they appear in all the different forms of love and hate. It is like and dislike that carry the soul to the intentional meeting with outer things and events; to the virtual images in the region of the mind as well as to the encounter in the sphere of the feelings and to the direct intercourse with things and beings in the field of willing.

All-embracing is the power of desire. It springs from the parts of the soul which are intimately connected with the bodily nature in which it lives. Here lies the region where the unconscious will-activities are situated and perform their service; from this dark well of our existence, desire emanates. It can be called a masculine quality.

The transcendent faculty is different. It permeates the discriminating process with creative power and tries to embrace and recreate all things and beings. We can imagine it as a feminine condition.

At last we must ask: In what way are these two attributes — the male and the female — related to one another? If we imagine correctly, we can understand that the radiating force of desire is an act of mental exhaling. The soul undergoes an expansion in the process of desire, while permeating the intentional qualities; its capacities exhale into the world around. The transcendent quality inhales again and takes the boundaries of the soul back to their own limits. This action brings about a concentration and a condensation within the soul and thus gives rise to the discriminating process.

Here we meet the most fundamental activity of the human soul: the process of breathing between the outer and the inner world. Desire is an act of exhaling, discrimination a process of inhaling. In the Greek mythology, the human soul was imagined in the figure of the goddess Psyche. She was accompanied by Eros, and in an imaginative way, the story of their love, their separation and ultimate union describes the interplay of these two faculties which live in our soul.

The story of Eros and Psyche tells us that the god appeared to the goddess in the veil of darkness; she is not permitted to see him and to recognize his divine form. Psyche, however, tormented by curiosity, lights the lamp when Eros is asleep and beholds his beauty. He then has to leave her and she sets out on a long and adventurous quest to find him again.

Eros is the image of the desiring quality, Psyche of the transcendent faculty of the soul. They search for one another and fail one another; they unite and are separated again; it is a continuous process of exhaling and inhaling, of expanding and contracting.

Synopsis

We have now discovered two new elements that work in the realm of the human soul. These two fundamental forces permeate our mental existence and are the foundation of the life of the soul. Just as ordinary breathing enables us to live our earthly life beginning at birth and ending at the gate of death, so does the mental breathing keep the soul astir and aware of the world. Eros exhales, and Psyche inhales.

The action of mental inhaling brings the mind into activity. Psyche lights the lamp in order to see and to know. But her gaze is burdened by her breach of the promise she gave; so is our mind engulfed by the sin we committed when through the Fall our 'eyes were opened'. Whatever the mind does, only virtual images of the world appear, and the discriminating power asserts their reality. In time, however, a new longing develops in the realm of Psyche; she yearns for the revelations of the spirit. She has to acquire the virtue of modesty to reach this aim.

The action of mental exhaling emanates from the realm of the unconscious. Eros arises and in the disguise of a serpent, he longs for Psyche. He tries to conquer the world in order to lay it at the feet of his bride. She, however, in breaking her solemn promise, drives him away and he has to leave her. But he cannot endure the 'divorce' and he seeks his companion again. In time, a new wish arises in the realm of Eros. He wants to suffer the earth and to endure human life in the darkness of destiny. He has to acquire the virtue of compassion to find his salvation.

Images now appear; the soul begins to speak of itself, to name itself and to describe its being. The following drawing is again an attempt to depict the phenomena which were described.

Chapter 3

Pain and Anxiety

The landscape of the human soul

Having surveyed the three regions of the soul, we made the attempt to describe some of the basic forces which create the fundamental web of all mental processes. We spoke of the transcendent quality in its relation to all cognitive abilities and we portrayed the intentional faculty as being connected to the sphere of desire. The transcendent quality was related to the region of the mind, whereas the intentional faculty was situated in the unconscious fields of the soul.

If we imagine these two regions, the mind and the unconscious, and realize their polar diversity, then a preliminary sketch-map of the soul can be laid out (p.38). The mind is permeated by the transcendent quality, thus enabling us to think, to remember and to recognize. The unconscious is filled with the power of desire which, in turn, initiates the intentional faculty.

The mind and the unconscious are realms and regions of the soul. Transcendent and intentional qualities, on the other hand, are formative powers. They provide the fundamental layers for the emergence of manifold experiences, conscious as well as subconscious ones.

Like a living body which consists of various layers, the soul also is formed of numerous spheres of structures and qualities. They weave into each other, merge and integrate and it is, therefore, very difficult to learn to distinguish the different patterns and forces.

The transcendent and intentional qualities are basic structures and without them no mental life is possible. They belong to the

Thinking

MIND

TRANSCENDENT QUALITIES

DISCRIMINATION

Feeling

LOVE   HATE

INTENTIONAL FACULTIES

DESIRE

UNCONSCIOUS

Willing

animal as well as to man. Both qualities weave the fundamental character of the soul's being; both are contained in each single mental process, in the same way that oxygen and hydrogen are present in every drop of water. In sense-perception, for instance, the intentional faculty leads the desiring soul to the object of perception; the transcendent ability grasps the image of the object and brings it home. It would be futile to imagine that any mental act can dispense with either intentional or transcendent forces.

They form, however, only a kind of substratum. The experiences, the deeds and suffering of the soul with all the manifold images appear as an ever-changing picture on the canvas of this substratum. Desire and discrimination, as we described them earlier (pp.33–36), give to this canvas the rhythmic faculty of inhaling and exhaling.

The soul is never at rest, never set, never finished. It is always alive, astir, active and changing — a moving panorama of forces, images, feelings and qualities. Whenever we try to hold it fast, it is quicker than our grasp and has again moved away. The soul is like a landscape, where day turns into night and morning into evening. The clouds come and go and the hills and mountains display their quickly changing colours. The sky and the ground are never the same. Rain and sunshine, hail and snow appear and dissolve. The trees and hedges grow year after year and change the face of the landscape. Some of the fields are covered with grass and others with corn. Winter changes into summer, birds return and leave again; their voices fill the air and disappear. The flowers grow, bloom and wither. What an amount of rise and fall, of life and death, of joy and pain fills a simple valley!

All this is like our soul; what we behold around us as the landscape of our daily life is, in another form within us, the manifold experience of our mental existence. For many who have to live in a town, the streets and their teeming chaos become their landscape. Townspeople try to create their individual landscape within their homes and rooms. With colours and flowers, with carpets and curtains, books and tables and pictures, the personal touch of the environment is created, so that the soul feels at home and is not completely starved to death.

Modern psychology suffers under the geat lack of imagination of its representatives. The psychologist of today lives, as a rule, in a busy street with cars and buses and trams; he, like his fellow men, no longer participates in the coming and going of the seasons, the waning and waxing of the moon, the rise and fall of the day. His experiences are narrowed down by men and man-made things; thus he loses the natural background of all existence. His psychology is as man-made as his surroundings. Mental experiences, as he imagines them, are as crude and straight and grey as a street in a suburb or a consulting room in a child guidance clinic. Heaven and earth are replaced by electric lights, testing utensils and concrete pavements.

Our task is to free ourselves from the strong imprint which these artificial products make upon us. We shall learn to behold anew the wonders of the soul in their manifoldness, their beauty and their constantly changing life. Our quest is now to discover some of the attributes of the landscape of the soul.

The problem of pain

One of these attributes is the experience of pain. Every human being knows it and to be in pain is a common condition to man. Yet, it is very difficult to describe this experience or to find an appropriate definition for this universal quality. Sir Thomas Lewis, in the preface to his book on pain, writes (1942):

> Reflection tells me that I am so far from being able satisfactorily to define pain, of which I here write, that the attempt could serve no useful purpose. Pain, like similar subjective things, is known to us through experience and described by illustration ... to build up a definition in words or to substitute some phrases would carry neither the reader nor myself any farther.

This is a very honest statement and we shall, to begin with, accept it. We know what is meant when we speak of pain. On the other hand, pain means such a variety of experiences, that we have to try at least to define its boundaries.

Another book on the same subject may help us to do this. It is also written by a Lewis, C.S. Lewis (1940), and appeared just two years previously to the other book. It deals with the same phenomena from an entirely different angle. Sir Thomas's book is purely scientific, having nothing else in mind but to search for the organic structures which enable us to have pain. The second book looks at pain from a purely religious point of view and tries to investigate the age-old question as to why pain and suffering exist at all. C. S. Lewis says:

> The truth is that the word Pain has two senses which must now be distinguished.

A. A particular kind of sensation, probably conveyed by specialised nerve fibres, and recognisable by the patient as that kind of sensation whether he likes it or not.

B. Any experience, whether physical or mental, which the patient dislikes. It will be noticed that all Pains in the sense A become Pains in the sense B if they are raised above a very low level of intensity, but that Pains in sense B need not be Pains in the A sense. Pains in the B sense, in fact, are synonymous with 'suffering', 'anguish', 'tribulation', 'adversity', or 'trouble', and it is about this that the problem of pain arises.

Lewis then states that his book deals only with pains of the B sense and does not concern itself with those of the A sense. On the other hand, Sir Thomas's thesis does not take into consideration anything else but the pain in the A sense.

Is this division altogether justified? Do these two types of pain really exist? Lewis says, very clearly, that pain is 'a particular kind of sensation' and that it is connected with certain nerve fibres. These sensations can be of various kinds as well as of various degrees. We distinguish piercing, throbbing, cutting, burning, dull and many other kinds of pain. We even distinguish between a pain, a sore, an ache and a smart, and describe with such expressions rather distinct experiences. It is a whole spectrum of pain which here reveals itself and each form has its own colour and shade. The intensity of a burning pain or a throbbing sore can be very different and immense varieties of possible pains exist. They are all experienced and they all give rise to anguish, suffering, trouble and tribulation. The latter sentiments are not another form of pain. The distinction made by C.S. Lewis is unjustified in the form in which he describes it; he throws cause and effect together. Pain is the cause of suffering and trouble; the latter are its result.

If I suffer the loss of one whom I have loved, I experience a dull ache of grief and pain. In such a case, I do not only experience a sensation of pain but also my reaction to it. This reaction is my suffering; the pain itself is my grief. All pains have rather similar sensations and reactions. If we hurt our finger by squeezing it in a door or window, we feel, to begin with, a pain which pierces through our whole body and it may even cause us to faint. We feel sick and sore all over. Later, the pain gradually localizes around the finger; it assumes a throbbing character and raises my awareness around the aching spot. If it is a severe pain, my mind turns to it continually. I then will try to avoid any movement in order to keep the finger quiet. I feel hurt, troubled and, in some way, offended. A host of feelings and emotions rise up on account of the pain and the ensuing suffering. After days or weeks, I am gradually restored to normality.

Many of the more common diseases are intrinsically bound up with pain and suffering and the 'patient' is the person who suffers. However it is not possible to identify illness and pain, except that they have very much in common. There can be illness without pain and suffering without disease.

If, after all these preliminaries, we approach the actual experience of pain, we may ask about the kind of mental quality it consists of. Is it a feeling, an emotion, a sensation? What is it really like? The French philosopher, Henri Bergson, once tried to investigate the experience of pain and his attempt is a very subtle one. He said (1919): 'Pain, as I believe it, is nothing else but the effort of the wounded organ to put things again into shape and order; it is a kind of motor tendency in a sensory nerve. Every pain, therefore, is an effort, but an effort in vain.'

Here the active side of the experience of pain is taken hold of. At the same time, it describes how this activity is thwarted and how we experience our weakness and inability.

A similar approach to the problem of pain is made by Rudolf Steiner. He describes, in one of his lectures ([1910 Feb 2] 1982, 1976), the following example. Suppose, he says, we have a special hobby which we particularly love to do, perhaps the daily watering of the flowers in our garden. One morning, however, we find that the watering-can has disappeared and we are unable to execute our task. 'You are distressed', says Rudolf Steiner. 'This is no physical pain, but, by being forced to dispense with a beloved occupation, you can almost experience a kind of physical pain.' He then continues to explain, that in a physical injury our mental powers have lost the possibility of using the organ which is hurt. In a similar way, as with the example of the lost watering-can, my soul 'experiences as pain and privation the inability to execute a common activity.'

Pain, according to both Henri Bergson and Rudolf Steiner, is the result of an inhibition, a privation, an inability to execute that which we usually perform. Therefore the loss of a friend, or even of a material object to which we are attached, creates the experience of pain. Pain is the symptom of loss. It is the result of a vain effort to restore something which we miss. Thus, Bergson thinks that pain 'is a motor tendency in a sensory nerve'. Here, however, he makes a great mistake as he does not distinguish between a mental experience and a physical organ.

We have already found that pain gives rise to suffering and anguish, to trouble and adversity. Now we see that pain itself is a result of privation through loss or injury. Here lies the reason for the common idea that pain is a kind of signal to warn every living organism of an impending danger. This kind of assumption has its root in the Darwinian concept of evolution. It is thought that life is a struggle for existence and survival and that most of our physical and mental functions are systems of aggression and defence. Therefore pain is supposed to be a relay system of warning signals. This is a complete illusion, without even a grain of truth. Pain is the result of physical, mental or spiritual loss and privation. In consequence it brings forth suffering, trouble and sorrow.

Something happens to us and the result is pain and a painful experience. This, in turn, gives rise to other emotions, feelings and moods. We may, therefore, present this complicated interplay in the following form:

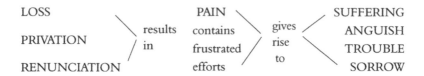

LOSS		PAIN		SUFFERING
	results	contains	gives	ANGUISH
PRIVATION	in	frustrated	rise	TROUBLE
RENUNCIATION		efforts	to	SORROW

This is a fair representation of all the manifold experiences and phenomena which are involved when pain occurs. But we return to our question: 'What is pain?'

The physiologist says (Wright 1952): 'Pain represents a special quality of sensation', and he adds: 'but it is charac-terised by a large emotional (affective) accompaniment.' The more advanced psychologists are not so certain whether or not pain is really a sensation. Some of them classify pain among the simple feelings and Buytendijk devotes a whole chapter in his outstanding book (1948) to this question of pain. He dis-cusses the 'pros' and 'cons' and, in the end, does not give a clear answer. However, self-observation and comparison with other mental experiences can only state that *pain is a sensation*. It can give rise to a manifold variety of emotions, motor reac-tions, feelings and other inner experiences but, in itself, it is a sensation. As such it is, however, distinctly different from many other sensations such as warmth and cold, touch and pressure, pricks and strokes. All these sensations can be accompanied by pain; they can even turn into pain if they themselves become too strong; yet pain is different from them.

If we ask the neurologist (Walsh 1957) where the experi-ence of pain has its physical organ, he will tell us that special nerve fibres are the mediators for the sensation of pain. All over the skin, in its upper and deeper layers, there are nerve fibres which apparently are specialized for the sensation of pain. The question as to whether or not every sensory nerve is able to experience the sensation of pain, is not yet solved. On the other hand, the great number of special nerves, which explicitly serve this sensation, has given rise to the idea that there exists a special 'sense of pain'. It is an interesting but cer-tainly a misleading idea. We must agree with Buytendijk who says: 'No sense of pain exists in the way that there exists a sense of touch or a sense of sight. The sensation of pain has, how-ever, its own quality which cannot be produced by intensifying other sensory impressions. Besides this, the sensation of pain is evoked by a special kind of nerve; yet there exists no sense of pain.'

This argument is not fully valid because it gives no reasons for the conclusion at which it arrives and it also does not mention certain characteristics of pain that are of great importance. We have already pointed out that the experience of pain can be greatly varied. A subtle self-observation and the many memories which all of us have will tell us that pain can not only be very manifold in kind but also in strength; and not only this. We can distinguish a highly pitched pain from a low and dull pain. We ascribe to the first a kind of piercing, dazzling experience, whereas with the other there appears to be a low, dark, brooding feeling. Here we meet the self-same qualities by which our colour and sound experiences are ordered. High and low, soft and strong, these are the varieties of sound, colour and pain. The different shades of pain compare very well with the various colours and many of us experience a burning pain as being red, a piercing pain as yellow and a dull pain as blue.

Aches and sores are often rather similar to sounds and tones and one may be entirely justified in saying, 'I hear the angels sing' when in very great pain.

We may describe all the possibilities of difficult pains as an orchestra or an organ of pain; but we may also call it an immense spectrum of colours. In this way, we become aware of the great universe of pain experience which has so many similarities to other sensory experiences, though it is different from them.

Here, however, we hold the key to the mystery of pain in our hands. The sensation of pain is no sensory experience in the true meaning of the word. It is more as well as less than this sensation. When we have pain, we experience a mental force which lies behind all the other sensory experiences. Pain is nothing else but the general quality of all other *specialized* sensory impressions. Behind blue and yellow, touch and heat, smell and taste and all the various tones and sounds lies a unifying, all-embracing force which makes the perception of them all possible. This substratum of sense perception rises up in us as an immediate experience when we are in pain. Behind all our sensory experiences stands the power of pain.

Rudolf Steiner once spoke about this general substratum. He said ([1924 June 27] 1981b, 55): 'Modern science speaks of light as of something that is present where we see things illumined. Spiritual Science speaks of light in another way. It calls "light" that which underlies other sense-perceptions too; it speaks, for example, of the light of perceptions of sound ...' Here we meet with the reality of pain. It is the light which weaves through all creation; the light which works behind all colours; the light which is imperceptible to us. All that we see is the result of this light. The true light itself remains invisible. In experiencing pain, however, we meet directly with this light and it pains us as we start to realize that it is the all-embracing, all-pervading universal power which has its centre in the sun.

Pain is light. And the experience of pain brings man face to face with the creator powers of the universe. Is it, therefore, a cause of wonder that in the centre of the cornea, opposite the pupil of the eye, we find the tightest and most exclusive gathering of nerves which are specialized for the experience of pain? This fact speaks clearly of the inner identity of pain and light. The painful power of a merciless, blinding sun is a revelation of this mysterious identity.

The enigma of anxiety

Perhaps no other mental phenomenon is more discussed today than the problem of anxiety. Gebsattel is quite correct when, in the introductory paragraph of his essay on the anthropology of anxiety (1954), he says: 'Anxiety has ceased to be the private concern of the individual. Western man lives in fear and anxiety; an undefined premonition of immense and oncoming menace shakes the ground of human existence. The importance of this phenomenon, which has steadily advanced in the course of the last hundred years, has now reached a level higher than ever before. Could it be, perhaps, that the capacity for anxiety of western man has continuously increased during the last three or four generations?'

Before going any further with our deliberations, it will be necessary to clarify the meaning of the word 'anxiety' and to distinguish it from the very similar experience of fear. This latter word hails from the Anglo-Saxon word *foer* which means 'a sudden peril' and 'an impending danger'. Once it was used in connection with the perils of travelling. Anxiety, on the other hand, is derived from the Latin *angustia* which denotes a condition of oppression or tightness. The German *Angst* is the same word and 'anguish' describes a similar state.

Anxiety is a kind of extended mood which overcomes us; it grows slowly but steadily upon us and can remain for days and weeks. Fear is more sudden and usually more intense and is, therefore, much more dramatic. Fear is a drama, anxiety an elegy.

William Stern, trying to distinguish between fear and anxiety, says (1928): 'We speak of anxiety (as distinct from fear), if we try to describe a general mood of diminished certainty. Such a mood need not be bound to an object which excites fear; it may appear without any obvious outer reason.'

The distinction between anxiety (*Angst*) and fear (*Furcht*) is of great importance. Fear is always related to an object; anxiety, at least to begin with, is not. Later, it can come about that anxiety is connected to an outer object and it may hang on to it very intensely. When anxiety occurs, it is like a general mood which has different shades of intensity. From a hardly noticeable dull feeling it can rise into an overwhelming emotion which not only irritates but sometimes deranges the suffering subject, the patient.

If we ask what the experience of anxiety is and what it means to be anxious it is not easy to give an appropriate answer. We know a great deal about the organic changes which occur in a state of anxiety; the change in blood pressure and heart-rate, the rise in the rhythm of breathing, the intensified muscular action of the whole of the intestinal tract and many more such signs are now well-known. It would be futile to argue whether such bodily conditions cause the mental experience of anxiety or vice versa.

The common state of anxiety is difficult to portray. It is a kind of sensation which arises over the whole body; it is connected with the feeling of a dark pall, a slight tension, a cloud which hovers above our feeling and thinking and throws a shadow over our mental existence. The rising anxiety permeates our personality almost completely and the organic changes increase with the intensity of the condition. Sweating, trembling, inability to move, palpitation, chattering of teeth, restlessness, diarrhoea and other signs, to a stronger or lesser degree, can accompany the mental experience of anxiety.

The individual is gripped by a state of confusion. Not only are his organs disturbed in their functions. A general condition of excitement moves the soul and permeates, at the same time, the bodily functions. It is as if the groaning outcry of all creation were resounding in the soul. We are usually quite unaware of the reason why anxiety has befallen us. We surrender to it in the same manner in which we surrender to pain. We are caught up in anguish and imprisoned in the dark room of anxiety. The meaning of the word expresses the experience; *angustia* means narrow, tight, a feeling of oppression, a fetter which cannot be loosened.

Behind anxiety stands the abyss of the unknown. Heidegger, the famous modern philosopher, coined the sentence: 'Anxiety reveals the nothingness.' The ground of our existence is swept away and we linger without goal or aim. We do not know of what we are afraid, but we are filled with uncertainty and, somewhere in the background, lurks death.

Loosli-Usteri expresses this experience in a very revealing form; she states (1948):

> A whole scale of reactions lies between the emotion of anxiety (in its deepest form always death-agony), and the feeling of fear (lastly always fear of God); ... it is no doubt one of the most beautiful tasks of education to lead the child in such a way, that it gradually learns to transform blind anxiety into reasonable fear. The fear of the Lord, not anxiety before him, is the beginning of all wisdom.

A state of anxiety is the condition of a world wherein education has failed to achieve this aim. The man of the present age is filled with anxiety for no other reason but this. Our educational system in the school, as well as in the family, has failed to transform the anxiety of death into the fear of God. Therefore, we have to face the constant rise in neurotic conditions which are the result of the insurmountable states of anxiety.

From birth on, anxiety lives in every human being. It rests in the valleys of our soul and shows its existence at any given moment. Stumbling, falling, a sudden fright, a condition of asthma, a foreboding dream, a dull feeling of uncertainty — they all lead to an anxious feeling. On the other hand, a mood of anxiety may arise without any apparent reason. Out of the depths of the unconscious it overtakes us and we become its slave.

We are justified in calling anxiety an emotion for it is similar to many other emotional conditions such as anger, hate, joy, grief, and so on. All of these are not actual feelings; they are both more and less than feelings. The fundamental form of feeling is either sympathy or antipathy. An emotional condition is much more powerful, much more dramatic. It is like a sudden change of weather in the landscape of the soul. A clear and beautiful day is suddenly altered by a rising storm, a shower of rain or other similar events.

Such an emotion is anxiety. It is a mist rising in our soul, a haze covering the horizon and gradually filling the whole land. The contours of things disappear and we can no longer find our way. Darkness envelops us; we are cut off from other beings. Heaven and earth merge into one another. The near surroundings assume hideous forms. A tree trunk appears as a crouched figure, a hump of earth as a wild animal. We have lost our articulation. What happens around us when fog develops, occurs within us when we are in a state of anxiety.

The question remains: from where does the mist of anxiety arise? We find again an answer when we remember a description which Rudolf Steiner once gave about the sense of touch. He does not speak of the sensory experience itself, but of all which lies behind it. He draws our attention to the spiritual background of this sensation when he says ([1920 Aug 8] 1985):

Actually, all that which lives in our sense of touch is also an inner experience, but this experience remains in the realm of the unconscious. Only a shadow of it appears in the qualities of touch, which are connected to our body. It is the sensory organ of touch which brings it about, that we are able to experience things as silky, woollen, hard or soft, rough or smooth. This radiates into our inner being; but we do not recognize this connection. This radiation into our inner being which is outwardly experienced as the sensation of touch, is nothing else but the feeling of being permeated with a dim awareness of divine presence.* Man would have no awareness of divine presence without the sense of touch. This power permeates all things; it also permeates our whole existence. It is the same power which bears and sustains all living beings. This all-pervading divine substance is, when we consciously realize it, the other side of our sense of touch.

Now we learn to understand the background of anxiety. This emotion is ultimately connected with the sense of touch because this sense enables us not only to experience our immediate physical surroundings, but also gives us an inner certainty. If we see an object or if we hear its sound, we are never quite certain of the value of its reality. As soon as we touch it, we are assured of its real existence. The sense of touch certifies to us the physical reality of a thing or being. In a similar way, it assures us of the Divine presence. The latter experience is not a conscious one, but occurs in the depths of our unconscious. It is one of the foundations of our life. We know of God because we experience his presence subconsciously, through our sense of touch.

To be anxious is the temporary loss of this fundamental experience. This loss is connected with a loosening of the soul from the physical frame of the sense of touch. Our soul is tied to the

* Rudolf Steiner uses here the word *Gottgefühl* which is not translatable; the rendering 'dim awareness of a divine presence' is an attempt to follow the meaning of this German expression.

whole of our skin. The sense of touch is like a harbour in which the ship of the soul is anchored. If the anchor is weighed, the ship drifts along without proper hold and the mist of anxiety rises. Any sudden experience, such as shock or fright or surprise, can bring this about. But also a gradual loss of faith, a continuous uncertainty as to the future, will unfasten the ground of our life, deprive us of the experience of Divine presence and thereby give rise to the appearance of anxiety. The mist of uncertainty lifts its wings and envelops the soul with its darkness.

Here we return to the concept of emotion. We called it a disturbance of the weather in the landscape of our soul. To begin with this was not more than an imaginative comparison, but now it is raised to a real image. Anxiety occurs when the soul drifts out of the harbour of the sense of touch. The ship leaves the land and heads into the open waters of the ocean. If there is no pilot who can direct the course, anxiety will appear. The waters change into fog and the sight is immersed in darkness.

Blind children live in a cloak of anxiety. No other person is so fundamentally given up to anxiety and fear as a blind person. Where the light, the view, the sight is missing, anxiety and fear appear. The sun dispels the mist; sight and clarity of vision obliterate the fog of anxious behaviour.

Sensations, like pain, are the children of the light or the light itself. Emotions, like fear and anxiety, are the children of the darkness or the darkness itself.

Synopsis

Another pair of mental forces has been described. An analysis of pain has led us to an understanding of sensory qualities and the study of anxiety has revealed the universal nature of emotion. Both belong to our soul; they are as inherent in our mental life as the faculties of transcendence and intentionality.

Sensations are the children of light. The various shades of light, its deeds and sufferings are not only colours, but all the different forms of sensations. Our simple sensory experiences, before they rise to become percepts, are these sensations.

Emotions are the children of the darkness. The different expressions of darkness, its gruesome and wholesome appearances, pervade our soul. They fill it with joy or sorrow, with happiness or with grief.

When Adam ate of the apple which Eve plucked from the Tree of Knowledge, his eyes were opened; his heart started to be overcome by fear and anxiety. Guilt was in his being and, when called before the throne of God, he confessed; 'I heard the sound of thee in the garden, and I was afraid, because I was naked; and I hid myself' (Gen.3:10). This was the first experience of anxiety. It was 'in the cool of the day' when it happened. The evening mist was rising and Adam knew for the first time what it means to die. The mystery of anxiety is the mystery of human death. The mystery of pain is the mystery of divine light. Both have their origin in the event of the Fall.

Images now appear; the soul begins to speak of itself, to name itself, to describe its being. Light and darkness live in the soul and build the soul.

Chapter 4

Fear, Shame and Anger

The language of the emotions

Our investigations into the 'Enigma of Anxiety' have opened up the study of the realm of emotions. This is a rather neglected sphere in modern psychology, although several attempts have been made to describe and characterize this vast field of human existence. We are all constantly under the direct or indirect influence of our emotional life. Many of our actions are determined and our decisions guided by strong emotional interests.

The landscape of our soul, as we have described it, is constantly changing through the play in its atmosphere; rain and wind and gales alternate with fine and lasting weather. At times the sky is overcast; on other days, a cloudless scene delights the eye. The rising mist of anxiety can be followed by the reassuring presence of a starlit sky. Meteorology in terms of the soul is the knowledge and description of our emotional life. Our emotions make our inner weather.

Modern psychology is still trying to understand the riddle of human emotions. The discovery of the unconscious has helped in understanding the problem better, but in other ways it has also led to many new difficulties and complications. What do we mean when we speak of emotions? Are they identical with feelings? Are they sentiments? What is the difference between emotions, sentiments and feelings? These questions are not so easily answered, and there are many varying views.

McDougall, for instance, writes (1923): 'Let us hold to the obvious fact that there are no such things as "emotions", any more than there are such things as "sensations" or "ideas" or "concepts".' This author is convinced that it is altogether wrong to speak of such facts as objects. We have emotional experiences, but no emotions; they, in McDougall's opinion, do not exist as entities at all. He includes in the general term 'emotional experience' such divergent mental qualities as fear, disgust, curiosity, lust, amusement, and so on, and thus veils, rather than clarifies, the order and appearance of emotions.

This is often the case with books and papers on psychology today. Different kinds of feelings, sensations, and even sense-perceptions are called 'emotions' or 'feelings' and it is very difficult to find the way through this thicket of nomenclature.

In another textbook on psychology (Woodworth & Marquis 1952), we read:

> Emotion is a 'moved' or stirred-up state of the individual. It is a stirred-up state of feelings — that is the way it appears to the person himself. It is a disturbed muscular and glandular activity — that is the way it appears to the external observer who sees the clenched fists and flushed face of anger and the tears of grief, or who hears the loud laugh of merriment and the pleading tones of love …
> Each emotion is a feeling and each is at the same time a motor set. Fear is a set for escape, and anger a set for attack … Emotion is also an organic state. The heart and stomach and other internal organs of the body are disturbed in emotion.

With this description we are one step further because we learn to understand the intrinsic connection every emotion has with the organic state of the body. It is, however, quite unjustified to say that 'the internal organs are disturbed' by an emotional experience. We can only say that they function differently from before. In a cat, for instance which is just digesting food, an angry feeling immediately stops the churning movements of its stomach and small intestine. A sudden state of fear in the human being creates pallor and sweat, and an irritated mind is usually accompanied by a change in the blood-pressure and an irregular process of breathing.

Thus we learn to understand that emotions are intimately connected with our bodily nature and that not only our feelings but also our whole organic condition is 'moved' and 'stirred-up'. It depends on the strength of the single emotion to what extent this stirring-up occurs. And there can be no doubt that emotions are very different in their extent and depth. Anger, for instance, can be but a state of annoyance, or it can rise to fury and rage. In a similar way, all other emotions have a certain spectrum or scale of appearance.

This, however, does not bring us nearer to a proper ordering of the different emotions. William James (1892) distinguishes between 'coarse' and 'subtle' emotions, and calls fear, love, hate, shame, grief and similar experiences 'coarse', whereas more refined emotional sensations such as may occur in religious, aesthetic and intellectual experiences, he calls 'subtle'. In connection with this division, McKellar writes (1952): 'A second distinction must be made between emotion and sentiment. Love and hate, though listed by James as emotions, would today be regarded rather as systems of emotional dispositions or sentiments.' And as 'sentiment' this author describes 'a whole range of emotional experiences in a variety of circumstances relating to the object'. He continues to classify sentiments in the following way: 'Positive sentiments such as love, liking and respect give rise to a range of sympathetic emotions towards the object; negative sentiments such as hatred, dislike and contempt lead to a range of antipathetic emotions towards the object.'

Here it already becomes quite obvious that what McKellar describes as sentiment is not 'a system of emotions' but rather a condition which gives rise to a display of emotions. To my mind it is quite unjustified to describe 'respect' or 'hatred' as a range of emotions. We may call such conditions sentiments, but we should never identify them with emotions or clusters of emotions.

The fundamental error underlying all these misconceptions is to be found in Darwin's essay *The Expression of the Emotions in Man and Animal*. Here the idea is expounded that all emotions are a kind of mental residue of much earlier conditions when the evolutionary struggle for existence persisted. Or as McDougall (1923) formulates it, that emotions are 'adaptations of the body to the modes of instinctive activity proper to the species. Each mode of instinctive activity requires, for its most efficient execution, the co-operation of all parts and organs of the body.' Thus McDougall and most of the psychologists concoct a connection between instinctive behaviour and emotional experiences, and they present us with equations like:

> Instinct of escape – fear
> Instinct of combat – anger
> Parental instinct – tender emotions, and so on.

These relations are quite unwarranted and simply the result of the Darwinian idea that life is nothing but the survival of the fittest. This unfortunate concept has veiled the true nature of our emotions and hindered an insight into their real being.

We have called emotions the 'children of darkness' in comparison to sensations as the 'children of light'. We shall only understand emotions if we see them as proper entities living in our souls, arising and subsiding like beings who awake and go to sleep again. Anger does not rise up so that I can put up a better fight and defeat my enemy; nor does fear arise in order to brace me up for my escape. Emotions do not occur to help or obstruct my daily life. The basic emotions are monitors for our Self in strange and unexpected situations. Emotions warn; they call and admonish and make us conscious of conditions of which we were not previously aware.

When we referred to laughing and weeping, which we described as 'emotional outbursts', we quoted Plessner's statement that 'we weep and laugh in a situation for which we find no other answer'. And we added: 'Instead of a rational answer, the reactions of weeping and laughing occur.' Here we meet with a fundamental insight applicable to every type of emotion. We now can state that emotions are answers without words to the questions put to us by special situations of life; emotions are a language without speech. They do not speak with words, yet they are very expressive. They are common to men all over the earth. The layer of our emotional life lies in the substratum of our unconscious; it is the remnant of an original speech which, once upon a time, unified all mankind. Before the 'Tower of Babel' was built, men did not speak in words but in emotional expressions, in gestures and in feelings. They all spoke the same primeval language. This was the time when we were still able to understand the song of the birds and the voices of the animals.

The remnants of this language still live in our soul. It is not I who speak it; my unconscious ejects this language — it calls on me, it shouts at me, it shakes me and warns me. It is a very forceful way of speaking and I cannot help but listen to it.

McDougall misjudges our emotional life when he ridicules the use of 'emotion' as a noun. Fear, anger, hatred, shame and all the other emotions as well as our emotional reactions such as laughing and weeping are individual entities in our soul. Each one of them has its special countenance; each is as different from the other as rain is different from snow, hail from thunder. Yet they all speak a language which can be understood immediately, by the one who experiences the emotion as well as by the one who observes the emotional outburst.

The meaning of anger

A general investigation into the nature of emotions will be fruitful only if it is followed up by a survey of the special forms of emotional life. To speak of 'emotions' is to characterize only very generally the specific sphere of the soul which reveals itself in the language of feelings, passions and sentiments. Each individual emotion has its own very peculiar appearance through which it unfolds. Fear is different from anxiety; anger is very unlike shame and courage. Nostalgia has quite specific features characteristic only of this emotion.

Anger is probably one of the most ancient emotions; it has a very special place among all other emotional experiences; it alone is ascribed to divine beings. The Old Testament speaks of 'the fierce anger of the Lord' in various places. It is quite familiar to us to imagine the anger of Zeus who throws his lightning into the wicked world, or to visualize Odin swinging the thunderbolt in divine wrath.

Language has several words for the whole spectrum of anger. McKellar (1952) speaks of an 'intensity series' and enumerates the following grades: irritation, annoyance, mild anger, intense anger, rage and fury. It appears rather questionable whether a condition of irritation or even annoyance are justifiably described as forms of anger. When I am irritated, I need not explode in an attack of anger; neither is being annoyed something to be compared with a real fit of mild or strong wrath. When I am simply annoyed, I feel irritated about something which has happened. I may be thwarted in one of my efforts or contradicted by someone who has a different opinion from myself. To be annoyed means to feel checked or stopped. Missing a train, or being hindered by help not given, brings about the feeling of annoyance.

We then experience ourselves as being alone, unwanted, not cared for, and we resent this attitude the world has displayed against us. When such instances repeat themselves several times in the course of a day, we may suddenly burst into a fit of anger. The latter is something quite different from the repeated experiences of annoyance. We become angry because we are in despair about the 'wicked world' which has turned against us. Anger usually arises as an act of despair. We are deeply upset and morally provoked about something we feel is unjustified, wicked or evil. This anger can increase and change into a form of holy wrath. On the other hand, it may sink into a storm of rage and fury. Anger itself, however, whenever it breaks out, contains an element of moral indignation of the highest form. Anger has something noble in its appearance. This is the lament of which Homer sings when he opens his great epic on the 'Wrath of Achilles'.

Anger is strong, it overcomes us in the way in which laughing and weeping possess us. Out of the depths of the soul it arises, heating our hearts, stirring up our feelings and we have to fight rather hard to remain master of the situation. We may clench our fists, show or set our teeth, raise our arms in despair, even tear up paper and break things. Anger will never move one person to attack another human being. We may hit out against an animal, we may even strike a child or destroy a lifeless thing.

We never fight against another person in anger unless rage and fury break out.

Annoyance, on the other hand, is different. It is hardly an emotion; it is an irritation, a disturbed equilibrium in the emotional sphere. Annoyance may give rise to anger; it can also give rise to resentment and hatred, to despondency and sorrow. Annoyance is like a seed which may develop into several possibilities of which anger is one. Annoyance is a form of grey; it has no proper colour, whereas anger displays a distinct tint.

Titchener (quoted in McKellar 1952), when he describes anger, points to the complex nature of this emotion. To him, anger contains 'the idea of the person with whom one is angry' as well as 'the idea of retaliatory action'. The condition itself he describes very dramatically: 'It begins with a feeling of displeasure, of pained surprise or wounded pride; but this soon gives way to pleasantness of anger itself, the delight in the idea of retaliation and the fact that one is strong enough to retaliate.' Here the 'idea to retaliate' is mentioned as part of the emotion itself. But anger is free of retaliation; anger does not think, it does not imagine, it does not wish to hurt. If such wishes occur, they are part of a sentiment which may appear as a result of anger. The angry person develops hatred against the sinner; the angry individual may be filled with the urge to destroy, but this is the result of the hatred, not the anger.

Having tried to distinguish anger from related sentiments and emotions, we may now ask: What is anger? What does it do to the human soul? Rudolf Steiner once spoke about the mission of anger and described the task of anger in the course of human evolution ([1909 Dec 5] 1984):

> Anger is a forerunner of something that is to appear at a later time. We first judge an event by anger in a more subconscious way; later on, we gradually learn — just through this unconscious judgment which anger enables us to make — to arrive at a more enlightened discrimination in the higher spheres of our soul. Thus in a certain realm, anger is like a teacher to man. Anger

arises as an inner experience long before we are ripe to
pass an enlightened judgment on something we feel
should not have happened.

When reading these sentences, we instantly think of
Plessner's statement that 'we weep and laugh in a situation for
which we find no other answer.' The same is true for the rise of
anger. It occurs in the moment in which we are unable to
change a situation or intervene in some event which we feel
should not happen. Anger is not a sign of might and strength,
but an expression of impotence. My helplessness in preventing
an injustice arouses my anger and wrath. It ascends out of my
soul like a glowing fire, fills me with disgust for and refusal of
the event or person that brought the event about. After a time, it
dies down, but it leaves remnants of hatred or distress, which
may also turn into forgiveness.

What is this anger which rises up and overcomes me and fills
my personality? Is it not like a thunderstorm which appears and
vanishes again after some time? Is not the thunder itself like
anger and the destructive power of lightning like rage? In the
landscape of our soul, annoyance and irritation gather like the
clouds before a thunderstorm. And like a thunderstorm anger
appears in us, takes its course, and dies away again.

Thus anger speaks without words. It arises, passes its judgment, clarifies the situation and then abates. It is a fatherly voice
that rings out through anger. This emotion always has a parental
character, and never is our wrath greater than when one of our
children is hurt or attacked. We are furious when a person we
considered our son or daughter casts aside his obedience. We
become angry when a thing which is ours is misused by someone else. Wherever our fatherhood is hurt or injured, anger
appears. This emotion is like a living father-image in our soul. It
is a seed of will, a nucleus of strength which can suddenly
unfold, permeate our being with the experience of wrath, and
die down again. It may turn into rage or fury if our conscious
personality fails to prevail and to hear the fatherly voice.

This living father-image is not a powerless picture such as
Jung's archetypes are. Anger is a reality, a power of will which

speaks without words but, nevertheless, with a strong voice. We do not hear this voice, but we feel it all the more. When anger arises in our soul, all the other qualities disappear before its majestic face. Likes and dislikes, thoughts and feelings flee into the furthermost corners of the land of the soul. Our ego stands lonely in the presence of anger. It feels like a child whose father has come to protect it. We accept his protection, his help and his strength. Therefore we behold Zeus and Yahweh and Odin in the image of their divine wrath.

The phenomena of fear and shame

Like anger or wrath, fear and shame are two distinct basic human emotions. We all know the experience of fear as well as of shame. They are different from other emotional experiences and unfold very specific qualities when they arise. We have already explained the difference between fear and anxiety and stated that fear is always related to an object. This is the fundamental difference between the two, for anxiety occurs without being directed towards something outside; it is a rather general emotion. Fear is a special one; it occurs during a specific situation and as soon as the condition has altered, fear disappears again.

Fear makes us shudder; we tremble, sweat and our teeth chatter in its grip. We turn pale and grow very tense and stiff. There is no urge or intention to flee because we are much too frightened to leave the piece of ground on which we stand. Fear has such a tight grip on us that we become immobile. It coils around our whole being as if it would crush our soul and body.

Shame gives us quite an opposite experience. Instead of growing tense and tight, we feel as if we would dissolve and melt away. Instead of growing pale, we blush over our face and neck, and sometimes even on the shoulders and upper part of the chest. We may, at the same time, sweat, but it is a warm sweat and not the cold we experience in fear.

These two emotions are polar opposite phenomena. Yet they belong together like day and night, or light and darkness. In fear, we shrink; the capillaries of the skin contract and the blood withdraws from the surface of the body. In shame, we expand;

the blood-vessels of the skin widen and the blood rushes to the surface of the upper parts of the body. It is a well-known fact that in some people, especially those who belong to races accustomed to living almost naked, the blush is more extended. It can sometimes go down over the arms and chest, even to the waist. Some cases are known of people even blushing over the abdomen and upper thighs (Mitchell 1905). These facts may indicate that in primeval times, man perhaps blushed all over his skin. In fear, we still develop a pallor all over the body.

Neither fear nor shame can be explained in a rational way. There is no obvious and known reason for the rise of these two very uncomfortable and most undesired conditions of our inner life. Both make something available to us which is unknown in our everyday existence. In fear as well as in shame, we stand face to face with an experience which suddenly arises. Something immeasurable opens up in front of us; it is as if the unfathomable background of all life and being would appear. Our thoughts begin to rush about like irritated ants. We feel guilty, we think of life and death, of God and our misdeeds. Our conscience plays havoc with our mind. We know that another completely new realm of existence has opened up, but we are prevented from having a clear insight into this new world. A door opens into a room which is usually forbidden ground. So sudden is this happening that we are frightened and hardly dare step near the threshold. And quickly the door is shut again.

Haensel says (1946):

> Fear has something tearing; opposite forces appear. This splitting-up tendency is the opposite pole to courage which has a gathering and concentrated power. Aristotle knew this, and he called fear a kind of oppression, a form of confusion. … The person who is in fear forgets himself, he not only tries to escape from the danger, he tries to flee from himself. … Fear is one of the emotional roots of religious concepts. Man approaches his Godhead with fear; if he fails to do so he acts frivolously and the divine wrath is evoked which makes him afraid.

In this deception, the experience of the 'Unknown' is presented. Fear appears to be a metaphysical event; it takes us to a threshold we are unable to cross. Fear makes us aware of the existence of this threshold, but not of what is beyond.

All these reflections now give rise to the specific question: When and under what circumstances does fear appear? A good deal of research has been done and I quote some of the results.

> The circumstances in which fear arises, even at a very early age, are so diverse that one cannot account for them simply by analysing the properties of the external stimulus ... It is difficult to find a common psychological ground or cluster of common subjective or internal factors that account for the various cases of fear ... Among the primary fears are fears of what is novel, strange and unfamiliar ... In addition to fears of unfamiliar persons, things and situations, fears have also been noted as response to unusual or 'uncanny' things, including some forms of mutilation. (Jersild 1954).

From these accounts, it becomes quite understandable that the 'Unknown' in the form of strange and unfamiliar things creates the rise of fear. On the other hand, it is well-known that some children and adults regularly experience fear when specific things happen. The sight of a dog or a cat can throw some children into a frenzy of fear. Solitude, separation, the crossing of a bridge, the locked door, a thunderstorm may create fear and fright in some people. These conditioned appearances of fear we call 'phobias'; they are present in a great number of persons and have their roots mostly in shock-experiences of early or later childhood.

What is this 'Unknown' which is so strongly bound up with fear? We called anxiety an experience of death, a kind of premonition of death-agony; it lifts us away from the ground of the earth and leaves us floating in mid-air. Fear, however, goes one step further. It is the prediction of the act of death itself and what will appear to us behind the gate of death. Anxiety leads us to the door; fear opens the door and makes us look at the abyss where death meets life. The shores of the river Lethe are the land of fear.

And shame? Where do we meet this very special and peculiar emotion? Mitchell says (1905):

> The state of mind during a blush, described broadly, is one of confusion ... The person who blushes has the feeling that his will is overpowered, and he is conscious of a sense of helplessness and flurry. He feels that his eyes are irresistibly borne down, and that he cannot look at the bystanders or bear to be looked at by them ... The stammering and stuttering of those who are blushing are often alluded to and have been frequently observed by myself ... The blusher seems to hide his head for shame. At least he avoids the gaze of the spectator ...

There is a Gaelic saying describing a girl who blushes — 'her face lit up with shame.' This description is rather appropriate because it refers to the 'inner light' we experience in a person who feels shame. We sense that this individual is overcome by a sudden bout of modesty; he recognizes his humble existence. It is mostly the young person who blushes; the older we become, the more we have done, accomplished and suffered, the less are we given up to the emotion of shame.

We must, however, distinguish between the act of 'blushing in shame' and the more inward feeling of 'being ashamed'. Both conditions are intimately connected, nevertheless they are different, not only in strength but also in quality. The state of 'blushing in shame' is a sudden involuntary emotion which overcomes the individual. The experience of 'feeling ashamed' is much more intimate and occurs in the centre of our soul, mostly without any outward sign. This second condition of 'feeling or being ashamed' has a moral quality; it is related to a feeling of guilt; we are hurt and subdued. The act of blushing in shame does not seem to carry any apparent moral value.

The word 'shame' is connected with the French word *chemise* which is the English 'shirt' and the German *Hemd*. All these words have their root in the Gothic expression *ga-hamon* which means 'to dress', 'to cover up'. Here the wisdom of the language reveals one of the secrets of the act of shame. We cover our face with a blush. Why do we cover ourselves?

Here we remember how Adam and Eve, when they had eaten from the Tree of Knowledge, suddenly 'knew that they were naked' and covered their nakedness with fig leaves (Gen. 3:7). We think of the experience of shame which befell the sons of Noah when they saw their drunken father lying naked in his tent. And Merell Lynd (1958) says in her very comprehensive essay: 'Throughout our western civilisation, shame is related to the uncovering of nakedness. The terms "Scham" and "Schamgefühl" in German carry the implication of uncovering nudity, and "Scham" is part of the compound words referring particularly to the female genitals.'

The 'uncovering' of other parts of the body can stir up the emotion of shame equally well. It need not be our own body, but also uncovered parts of other bodies make many people blush, because something which should remain hidden is suddenly exposed. And Merell Lynd remarks quite rightly 'that this public exposure of even a very private part of one's physical or mental character could not in itself have brought about shame unless one had already felt within oneself not only dislike, but shame for these traits'. In a different part of her investigation, the same author says: 'The shameful situation frequently takes one by surprise. But one is overtaken by shame because one's whole life has been a preparation for putting one in this situation. ... *I am ashamed of what I am.*'

In this statement, we hold the key for the understanding of the act of shame: 'I am ashamed of what I am!' In a most lucid representation, Anders (1956) refers to shame as an event in which man is confronted by a higher judge than himself; this higher court reveals to him something he does not want to be, yet is inescapably condemned to be. The author refers to a hunchback who feels publicly ashamed for being the one who has the hump. He is ashamed of being what he is. For him, too, his 'whole life has been a preparation' for making him ashamed.

But what makes a young man or woman suddenly blush? In them a similar experience occurs. They also feel ashamed of what they are. But, we may ask, of what are they ashamed? To blush in shame means to stand face to face with one's own self. A sudden recognition of one's humanity and one's human existence arises. We realize that we were born naked and that we have entered this life as poor and helpless sinners. This is the immediate awareness that lives in the background of blushing in shame.

As Adam and Eve 'knew', discovered and experienced their nakedness, so do we 'know' of our birth which put us into this earthly life. 'I am a creature, born and created' is the hidden realization behind every act of shame. Just as my head was thrust out into the open from my mother's womb and my breath sucked in the surrounding air when my lungs expanded for the first time — so do I blush and cover my face in shame. Every act of blushing is, in the depth of my unconscious, a memory of the unique moment of birth. Blushing brings home to us the tragedy of being born; of being sent into this world, naked and sinful.

If we had never before heard of the Fall of Man, fear and shame would have shown us the reality of this event. In every one of us the sudden realization that came to Adam and Eve is continually present. Birth and death are harboured in the depths of our soul. When danger appears, death arises in the form of fear. When we are taxed by meeting other human beings, birth arises in the form of shame. Between these two, we try to steer the ship of our destiny. Every man stands between these two experiences which are prepared to arise at any moment of our life on earth.

Three companions: fear, shame and anger

In the introductory chapter of this essay, we came to the conclusion that human emotions speak a language without words. When we find ourselves in either an outer or an inner situation for which we have no reasonable answer or rational understanding, emotions and sentiments will arise. They give the answer and react on our behalf. Our mind, overcome by an event, withdraws, and emotions speak instead. But are emotions which so suddenly appear not also part of ourselves? Or are we able to distinguish between our Self and our Emotions?

Modern psychology, especially under the influence of Freud, has come to distinguish between the various layers of the actual personality, or individuality, of man. Freud and his followers speak of the 'ego', the 'id' and the 'super-ego'. As ego they describe 'the lasting or recurring continuity of the body and mind in respect of space, time and causality' (Quoted from Lynd 1958). 'The id is the primordial reservoir of energy ... derived from the two primary life and death instincts. It is completely unorganised, thus differing from the ego of which organisation is the hallmark' (Jones 1957). The super-ego is 'a vastly important element of human nature, an element, however, which is itself largely unconscious' (Flugel 1945). The super-ego is a kind of judge who continually watches and censures our deeds and thoughts.

This distinction between these three layers of our personality is a very artificial one. It simply shows modern psychology's lack of insight into the true being of man. The id has no connection with our ego whatsoever; it is part of our emotional life and existence; it harbours drives and instincts which form a collective sphere for all human beings. The ego is identical with the experience of our own personality. It is the result of our memories, our thoughts and our sense perceptions. The 'super-ego' in the Freudian conception is completely unreal. It is similar to our conscience, but includes our ideals, our vanities and the illusions we all have about ourselves; it is a mere concoction wilfully mixed.

Rudolf Steiner, however, revealed the true nature of the ego and the so-called super-ego. He calls the ego the lower and the super-ego the higher self. When we are born, we leave our higher self on yonder side of the gate of birth and, with our soul, we enter into the earth-existence. In the course of the first years of life, we gradually take hold of our body. In the meeting between soul and body the lower self develops; it grows with the growth of our body and with the amount of experience the soul undergoes. Rudolf Steiner says ([1913 Aug 29] 1982):

This lower self which man has in the physical world is
the sum total of all the experiences which consist of the
sense-perceptions we receive in the physical world and
the results of what our soul develops in thinking, feeling
and willing here on earth. The higher self, on the other
hand, 'inspires our destiny'. Our experiences of joy and
sorrow are inspired by our higher self from out of the
spiritual world.

What is meant by this is that our higher self guides our life
through joy and sorrow from one stage of destiny to the next
from beyond the gate of birth. This higher self is like a higher
being which shows us our way through life on earth. Between
birth and death, we are severed from this higher self. However,
it still knows of us — even though we ourselves are quite
unaware of its presence. After death, we again unite with our
higher self.

In fear and shame, however, we dimly grow aware of it.
When we blush, we feel our naked birth with bashfulness and
our face 'lights up'. We cover our face in shame but it lights up
because shame is a comforter who speaks: 'Behind your nakedness appears your real being, your higher self.' In shame, we
look back to the gate of birth.

In fear, when we grow cold and stiff, we look forward to the
gate of death. We suddenly become aware of the transitory state
of our existence here on earth. Fear reminds us of our death, but
also of our ultimate reunion with the higher self. We all remember how much we liked, as children, to get the 'creeps' and to
shudder. This was because a strange element of satisfaction is
connected with fear. We were then experiencing the other side
of fear — it spoke of our end, telling us that it would be a new
beginning, because the arms of our higher self would lovingly
receive us back again.

Shame and fear are the two guides of our lower self, they
keep it constantly in touch with its higher being. Shame and fear
are like the borders of our mind and consciousness. As soon as
an incident or shock throws our daily life out of order, fear as
well as shame appear, speak their admonishing language, warn

us, and then withdraw again. These two kindly beings accompany our lower self until it has gained enough strength to manage without them: to be able to meet a danger without the fear of death, and to meet self-recognition without the blush of shame.

We can now visualize both fear and shame as the two relatives of anger. In the same way that anger appears when we are not yet able to judge a situation according to its moral value, so do fear and shame arise to speak instead of us when life presents us with events for which we are not strong enough. Fear, shame and anger are our good companions. Before us walks anger, guiding our moral judgments. At the right side goes fear, at the left, shame. They never appear unless we are in need of them. They are the three good servants of our higher self; they give their help as long as the lower self is in need of it.

Our unconscious being harbours these three companions; they are waiting in the shadow of the depths of the soul. The depth itself is filled with the power of anxiety. We can now imagine our individuality, the lower self, led by anger, held by fear and shame and treading on the ground of anxiety. These are the four great emotions that accompany every one of us throughout our life on earth.

Synopsis

Three further powers of the human soul have now been described. They are three guardians and helpers of the lower self on its way from birth to death. All three, together with their great and mighty sister, anxiety, originated at the moment of the Fall.

After Adam and Eve had eaten the fruit of the Tree of Knowledge, they began to realize their nakedness. In this moment of shame, the reality of death appeared before them and fear gripped their being. The tragedy of birth and death became true.

And God in his mercy bestowed a small morsel of his wrath upon the two sinners who, since then, are endowed with the gift of anger.

When Adam and Eve left paradise, they were accompanied by fear and shame, and anger walked before them. And the words of the angel rang in their hearts: 'I shall ye slowly both recall.' The children of Adam and Eve have learnt to understand that paradise will again be opened to them when their souls have become transformed.

When anger has changed into love,
shame has turned into hope,
and fear has metamorphosed into faith.

Images now appear; the soul begins to speak of itself, to name itself, to describe its being. The soul enshrines the whole becoming of man.

Chapter 5

Mood and Temperament

The human moods

Emotions are the companions of the human self. We harbour them in the unconscious depth of our soul and they are ready to appear in moments of stress and need. They withdraw as soon as a fair amount of equanimity is re-established and our self is again able to manage the situation.

Emotions have a quick and passing existence. They occur suddenly, assume their full strength within a few moments and die away in a short time. To be caught by fear or anger, shame or anxiety, is like an attack or a seizure. We are suddenly gripped by the outbreak of one of these great emotions and our whole existence succumbs under their powerful onslaught. Anxiety can last for a longer time, but fear, shame and anger usually disappear very quickly. They are like cloudbursts and thunderstorms in their coming and going.

Besides these major emotions, the soul is continuously permeated by a set of minor sentiments. We have already described the state of irritation and annoyance which may precede an outbreak of anger. We may also experience a fearful or anxious condition for a number of days, or we may sometimes be fretful or ill-tempered. These minor emotions or sentiments are the moods of the soul. They can last for a considerable time and tinge the basic attitude of our daily life.

Moods can suddenly arise and usually stay on for many hours or even days. An outer impression is able suddenly to change our mood. A beautiful landscape, for instance, or a piece of music, a song or a friendly word can help us to overcome a depressive mood. On the other hand, a happy disposition can be changed into a sudden outbreak of melancholy by a sad melody or a tragic event in our surroundings.

Moods are 'states of mind' which come and go with much less speed than emotions do. Moods are also less powerful; they are a kind of undertone which influences our soul, a disposition which gives a certain colour to everything we do and suffer, but does not overcome us as do the emotions.

Goodenough says (1945): 'A mood is not an emotion but a state of readiness, a "set" towards some particular kind of emotional reaction.' And McKellar (1952) believes that 'moods are affective states, typically of low intensity and longer duration than emotions.'

To understand the difference between mood and emotion is of great importance, as otherwise we would not be able to achieve an appreciation of mood as a 'state of mind'. Emotions are sudden outbursts; moods are lasting, and our soul is always under a special mood. The affective disposition gives to the soul its very special and personal colour.

The word 'mood' stems from the Old English *mod* which meant 'mind' or 'heart'. It thus corresponds to the German word *Mut* which in its ancient meaning pointed equally to the word 'heart' or 'soul'. Today the word *Mut* has changed its meaning and expresses 'courage', whereas 'mood' in German is *Stimmung*. This latter word may help us to grasp the meaning of mood in a new way. *Stimmung* derives from the verb *stimmen* and its significance is similar to the English very 'to tune'. We tune an instrument to make it sound higher or lower. The different strings are tuned in such a way that their tension is heightened or lowered and the word 'tune' itself derives from the word 'tone'. The 'tone', however, is the 'mood' of an instrument.

We now begin to understand that our mood is a condition of the soul which is comparable to the tuning or the tone of an instrument. The soul is either in a low or a high mood according to the way in which it is tuned. We may be in an aggressive mood if we are tense and 'high pitched'. Or we may be in a low mood if the tone of our soul is flat and the strings are loose and unable or unwilling to produce a melody.

Thus mood is a general state of our soul. It is not a special element or a new and singular quality of sentiment. It is much more the inner experience of a condition which we so easily observe outwardly in other people. Usually we sense at once whether a person is in a bad or a happy mood. We 'feel' it because our soul resounds to the tone of the other person's frame of mind. If we are in a happy mood and someone enters who is ill-disposed, we feel the disharmony at once and are irritated. This disturbance may give rise to annoyance or even to anger.

If, on the other hand, a friend who is in a happy mood visits us when we are morose or unwell, a similar disharmony will occur. Our friend may change our frame of mind if he tries to dispel the dark clouds which hang around us. But he may also achieve the opposite and drive us into deep and lasting despair.

These few examples are everyday experiences which reveal to us the transitory character of our moods and the great influence which other people's frames of mind have on our own 'tuning'. We continuously respond to this subtle influx. On the other hand, we ourselves influence the people around us by our own mood. Waves of ill and good temper permeate our daily existence. We all remember incidents where a party was swept by a gay mood and everyone present felt happy and elated. But we may also recall events where an audience or an assembly was especially ill-disposed and a single word could give rise to an outbreak of temper or aggressive shouting.

Thus we recognize that mood is not just a personal experience which is confined to the boundaries of our soul. It is a general state of interpersonal relationship and as such carries great weight in the life of the family as well as of the community at large. On a 'moody' day, the family may be in deep despair and tension runs high among its members. The following day, however, things may have changed and the sun will shine again. An ill-tempered father may destroy a cheerful atmosphere and restore it again after a good meal. The swing of life goes up and down like light and darkness.

We would make a vital mistake if we assumed that happiness or sorrow are already in the spectrum of mood; this is by no

means the case. A good mood can induce happiness and a bad
mood may give rise to sorrow. Mood in itself is only the condition under which these two qualities of our soul can appear.

We must also clearly distinguish between mood and temperament. To be melancholic or phlegmatic, choleric or sanguine, is different from being in a mood. The temperament is
an innate disposition which a person carries throughout his life.
We may define the temperament as the dispositional mood of
the individual. It is the reactivity and sensitivity of a person
towards the world. The temperament is innate and hardly
changeable. We may learn to control it but basically it remains
with us throughout life.

Thus we have to distinguish between three different forms
of mental qualities which bear a deep relation to one another:

— The quick living emotions,
— the slow changing moods, and
— the lasting temperaments.

All three have their special characteristics and their peculiarities and we shall try to describe their differences as well as their
similarities.

Emotion, temperament and mood

The science of the four human temperaments originated in
Greece. It was especially Hippocrates who described in some
detail the melancholic, phlegmatic, sanguine and choleric temperaments. This great physician, the founder of scientific medicine, based his theory on the idea of *krasis* and *dyskrasis*, the
harmonious and disharmonious mixture of the four humours of
the human body. According to his teaching, these four humours
which he interpreted as four different fluids are closely related to
the four temperaments. Too great an amount of 'black bile'
induces the melancholic temperament. An excessive production
of 'yellow bile' makes a person become sanguine. The 'phlegm'
— a kind of lymph — is related to the phlegmatic, and the blood,
the fourth humour, is the creator of the choleric temperament.

'The body of man,' says Hippocrates, 'has in itself blood, phlegm, yellow bile and black bile; these make up the nature of his body and through these, he feels pain or enjoys health. Now, he enjoys the most perfect health when these elements are duly proportioned to one another in respect of compounding, power and bulk and when they are perfectly mingled.' (Quoted from Castiglioni 1946).

For more than two thousand years, the idea of the four humours remained the foundation of medical thinking. In the course of the last century, it was gradually superseded by the modern concept of cellular pathology and biochemistry.

Hand in hand with this loss, the idea of the four temperaments also vanished. Modern psychology, in so far as it still has a more human side, is just willing to mention the facts of the temperaments. In most textbooks, however, no remarks are made any longer on this 'ancient' subject. Only recently have some of the German psychologists tried to revive this old teaching again. Gruhle (1956) for instance, writes, 'Temperament, so people say, is the realm between body and soul; it is physical in so far as it is steered by the soul, or it is mental in so far as it expresses itself in the body.' The latter is not so much to be seen in our gestures as in the pattern of our movements. 'Whether somebody's tempo in walking and working, in his speech and in his recreations is slow or quick, or if his reactions are hasty or lethargic, also if his speech is loud or low and whether he says a lot or very little ... these and some other forms of his affective behaviour cannot be categorized in any other way.'

Here, Gruhle points out that we need the idea of the temperaments in order to describe certain distinct features of human behaviour. He quotes the statement of Kerschensteiner who calls temperament 'the biological character or the biological individuality' of a person.

From such quotations it becomes quite obvious that the temperament is intimately connected to the bodily nature of man. The state of our physical condition has a definite influence on our temperamental behaviour. But it would be wrong to conclude that the flow of our blood or the production of bile can cause a choleric or sanguine temperament.

We can only gain a real concept of the four temperaments if we see them work in the realms of both mind and body at the same time. Temperaments influence our mental as well as our physical qualities. They induce the various forms of our reactive behaviour, our irritability, our perseverence. They are altogether able to modify and to determine the reactions of a person towards his surroundings. The four temperaments are the patterns of our conduct and our attitudes.

Rudolf Steiner paid great attention to the teaching of the four temperaments. He once said ([1909 Jan 9] 1928): 'The essential riddle of man's existence expresses itself in the temperament; it is the keynote of his being.' And he describes how the temperament keeps the balance in man 'between his inherited qualities and those abilities which are contained in his innermost being'. Rudolf Steiner explains how the temperament stands between the temporal and the eternal part of the being of man. The relationship between his higher and lower self — in so far as the lower self is more his biological nature and his higher self the mind and mental qualities — is expressed in the temperament.

The reality of the temperaments cannot be understood without their relation to time. They are basically rooted in the flow and the rhythm of time. That which is timing in music is temperament in man. A melody may sound quite different if its rhythm is changed from quick to slow. Its impression will vary with its tempo. The same sequence of tones when played at different speeds or rhythms will produce quite diverse reactions.

We may therefore say that the tempo and rhythm in the flow of our mental qualities as well as our biological constitution is determined by the inborn temperament of our personality. This is not identical with our constitution, nor is the temperament a quality of our soul. It is the innate time-beat and rhythm of our existence.

Different from temperament are the moods of our soul. They are by no means a constant and unchangeable constituent of our behaviour. Moods come and go at a comparatively slow pace; they rise and vanish away.

The temperament gives the personal note to every individual. It is specific in its form and function. Any one of the various moods, on the other hand, is somewhat the same in different people. We all experience the same sensations and create the same impressions on our surroundings when we are in a certain mood. Whether prince or farmer, teacher or pupil, master or servant, we suffer or enjoy the same types of moodiness. A well-educated person may be able to hide his ill temper better or give less expression to his happiness than someone who is uneducated. The moods and sentiments are, however, identical.

We may sometimes be inclined to forget the difference between mood and temperament. We may take a low mood as an expression of a melancholic temperament, but these two are fundamentally different. A melancholic person need not be in a bad mood. He is introverted, sullen and introspective. We would misjudge him by calling his conduct a sign of moodiness.

An ill mood may alter the tempo of our movements; it may thereby influence our temperamental rhythm. The mood itself is never the rhythm; it can modify the timing of our gestures or the speed of our walking. We move rather slowly in a dark room but quicken our steps when the light is on. The mood is a matter of light or darkness. The low mood is like a mist, rising up in the landscape of the soul. It is also like a cloud. A good mood is like the light of the sun which permeates the atmosphere. Mood comes like dawn and dusk and invigorates or depresses the forces of our life and our soul.

The light outside is like the joy within; the darkness outside is the depression within. Between joy and sorrow, happiness and depression moves the scale or spectrum of our moods. There is no tempo or rhythm as there is with the temperaments. The space which is filled with light or dusk is the image of our mood; every landscape transfers its mood into our soul and we often transmit our inner mood into our surroundings. Mood is related to the space within our soul and to the world which surrounds us.

There can be no question that mood is deeply connected to our physical condition. Not every illness, but certain disorders make us feel very uncomfortable and low. A stomach upset, a severe headache, a dull pain will create a depressive mood. We succumb to the physical discomfort and are no longer in tune with ourselves.

If on the other hand, we enjoy a period of health and fresh-
ness, for instance, after several days of rest and sunshine, we feel
at one with our self and our body. The inner light of our ego
permeates the body with strength and is in complete harmony
with it. This condition is a pure joy when the sun of the self
radiates through a cloudless soul and shines on the hills and
meadows of our body.

There is, however, equally no question that moods are
brought on by a mental upset. An angry exchange of words or an
inappropriate remark by a person against someone we like may
quickly cloud our inner horizon. Whether we feel well or
unwell will create a good or a bad mood. It is even possible that
the continued hostility of some people who dislike us may be
instrumental in making us ill. Many diseases are the result of
such an injury. Then the ego withdraws or it remains fixed to
the continuous aggression and does not find its way out of this
tangle of ill will. Such a person may drown in his own dark
mood and destroy the health of his body. Our organs and tissues
need the light of our self as nature needs the light of the sun.
Both become ill and miserable if the light does not shine. The
sun and the self are equal to one another. Both rule the realm of
the moods, inside and outside.

Light and darkness give the tension and the tone to our soul.
Just as our muscles can move only if a certain amount of tone
keeps them alert, neither will our soul move without tone and
tension. The light of the self gives courage (*Mut*) to the soul.
The loss of this light makes the mist of the unconscious rise
and the tone slackens; indifference and apathy are the consequence.

Emotions appear suddenly and disperse again very quickly.
They come and go like helpers, warners and wardens; they are
equal to our self. They occupy the space of our soul to such an
extent that our ego is left with little room to itself; it is almost
wiped out while we are in an emotional state.

Somewhere we know of our anger, our fear, our shame, our
anxiety. But we are rather helpless because each single emotion
has us in its grip like an animal its prey. The emotion shakes us
and leaves us thoroughly exhausted after it has disappeared.

After a fit of anger or fear, we need some time to recover and collect ourselves again.

Emotions are not comparable to moods or temperaments; they are of an entirely different quality because they are qualities in themselves and not conditions or dispositions like moods and temperaments. It is a fundamental misjudgment of modern psychology to throw all kinds of emotions and passions, moods and feelings into one big barrel which it names 'affective behaviour' or 'emotions'. Some psychologists even deny altogether that emotions and feelings exist (for instance, Hillman 1960).

What is necessary is to distinguish again between the various realms of the human soul. It is a vast kingdom and we should always remember the words of Heraclitus which we quoted at the beginning of Chapter 2.

The mechanism of different moods

We have just made an attempt to understand the special character of our moods and we found that their spectrum extends between joy and misery, which we compared with outer light and outer darkness. Now we have to ask a further question: From what place within our soul does this light or darkness emanate? Are there special regions in the land of the soul which make it possible that moods appear and vanish?

In the diagrams at the end of Chapter 1 and at the beginning of Chapter 3, we distinguished the realm of the mind and the sphere of the unconscious. They were described as the two poles of the soul: the upper and the lower. We found that between these two lies the region of our feelings. Do moods emanate from any of these three realms of our soul?

We already mentioned that moods are not entities in themselves. They are our soul's reactive behaviour to many different influences which disturb the even tone of our inner life. Such influences lower or raise the equilibrium of the soul's general mode. If they occur, the balance between mind and unconscious is deranged and the soul reacts by altering its general tension. Whence do these disturbances come? They occur within as well as without. Sense-impressions, memories, new ideas, subtle influences from other people and many other influences may be at work. Our soul is like a highly sensitive recording apparatus which registers all these diverse impressions.

Intimate self-observation may teach us a most important insight into the mechanism of moods. If one morning, we find ourselves especially moody and try to discover the reason for our discontent, we may suddenly find that our head is dull and aching. As soon as we make this discovery — in spite of continued headache — our mood may change and give way to inner tranquillity. Our early moodiness arose because our mind and consciousness did not register the disturbing influence: the pain and dullness in our head.

In every instance of bad mood, we shall find the same kind of pattern. Something has penetrated the soul's domain and has invaded the region of the mind without our noticing the intruder consciously. We feel uneasy, disturbed and irritated, but do not know the reason for it. We experience the irritation and uneasiness and call it a bad mood, but we do not discover the cause of it. It is like a dark cloud on the otherwise clear sky of our consciousness.

Many such clouds gather in the course of a single day because impressions from all sides permeate our mind. In many instances, these clouds dissolve as quickly as they formed. When we are walking or driving along a road, thousands of percepts are absorbed without being registered. Many of them dissolve; others sink down into the unconscious and only a few turn into memories. None of these give rise to any kind of mood.

When, however, an experience of some import is repressed into the unconscious — for one or the other reason — we will at once start to feel uneasy and moody. We are equally disturbed and under pressure when we fail to recall a name or an incident. How depressing it is to have forgotten the name of a friend or the title of a book we have just read!

These few examples can clearly explain that ill mood, tension and irritation are often the result of our inability to take hold of something consciously which stirs in the depth of the soul. Here lies one of the main causes of moodiness.

There is, however, the other side of mood — when we are happy, bright and full of joy. This condition is the opposite of a bad mood. To feel 'on top of the world' means to have the whole world in the grip of our consciousness. Our limbs obey our orders; we feel strong and able to meet almost any obstacle. We see and hear, we move and run as the master of our body and mind; we are truly 'on top of the world'. In such a state, we are conscious enough to resist any mental or emotional intruder. The sun of our mind is brightly shining and able to spot any interference.

The two forms of mood — the light and the dark — are stages of consciousness. A person who has difficulty in waking up in the morning will be in a low mood; everything will irritate him and be a disturbing factor until such time as his mind has gained control over his semi-consciousness. It is similar in the evening when we get tired and sleepy but have to do some work or listen to a lecture which does not interest us. In this case, we will become moody, irritated and fidgety.

And now we are ready to ask again: How does moodiness occur? Which kind of mechanism is responsible for the appearance of the different forms of mood? Are we able to answer this important question?

Impressions reach the soul by means of the senses. From the world around as well as from the frame of our body, perceptions pass through the senses to our mind. The lower senses such as the sense of life, the sense of movement and the sense of equilibrium give us a certain experience of the condition of our body.

Through the sense of life we receive a dull awareness of the functional condition of our organs; our feelings of well-being or discomfort are related to this sensory sphere. The sense of movement makes us aware of the positions which the different parts of our body have towards each other. This sense conveys to the mind an impression of the way in which our arms and hands, feet and legs move or relax. The sense of balance permits us to experience our upright position from the head downwards in the three dimensions of outer space.

The higher senses give us the impressions of the outer world. Colour and sound, smell and taste, warmth and cold become constant perceptions of our mind and soul. We receive these sensory experiences as a manifold source of information from morning till night. Only when we are asleep are the doors of our senses closed, allowing but few impressions to reach our mind.

The senses, however, have a twofold function. They are not only receivers for outer stimuli but are to a very high degree guardians against too many and too strong impressions. The latter function is largely disregarded though it is at least as important as the receiving part. Especially the senses of life, movement and equilibrium are a powerful barrier against all those forces which keep our body alive. We are unaware of the main processes going on within our organs. We do not experience the physiology of digestion and the vital powers of metabolism. The flow of the blood, the action of our heart, the activity of our muscles — all these functions are hidden from our mind. Only when we are unwell, in pain and discomfort, do we start to experience the activity of our organs. In such conditions, the barriers of our bodily senses are pierced and overrun. As soon as this happens, intruders of all kinds penetrate the realm of the soul and create the clouds of moodiness.

A similar process occurs if too many impressions, too strong sensations or too quickly changing perceptions reach our outer senses. A constant humming noise, a piercing cry, a blinding flash, a penetrating smell are likewise too much to be borne and tolerated. Our sensory organs succumb under the impact of the many and too strong sense-impressions which modern life produces, because their threshold of endurance is overtaxed. Thousands of sense-impressions reach our mind without control at the sensory border. They are the 'hidden persuaders' who roam through our mind — undiscovered and unwanted strangers. They make our soul tense and irritable. Here lies the cause for our moody generation. We have become nervous and neurotic, because the number of unobserved and unheeded sense-impressions is so enormous that we no longer have the possibility to digest them. Huge masses of unused images fill the soul and cloud the light of the mind and consciousness.

Thus the fundamental borderline between the soul and the world is riddled, and through the hollow spaces pours the mist of anxiety. It creates darkness in the region of the mind and the soul tries to counteract this invasion by making itself tense.

The immediate result is restlessness, tension and sleeplessness. The next step is a deep-seated irritation which makes the mind search for more impressions, stronger stimulations and greater agitation. This is the reason why people of today become so easily annoyed and difficult in their relations to others. Moods instead of the light of the mind fill the souls. The reactive behaviour loses its personal colour and the individual temperament is shrouded in the mist of nervousness, haste and irritation.

The only help for such a condition are days of complete rest and withdrawal from sense-impressions. Then it is possible for the soul to assimilate gradually the 'hidden persuaders' and to seal off again the frontier of the senses.

Unlike the emotions which appear out of the realm of the unconscious, moods are part and parcel of the surrounding world and of our body which infiltrate our soul. They go round the portal of the senses and appear as pain and pressure, as undigested and unrelated sound and smell, noise and cold, warmth and touch.

A later generation will learn to understand that this over-stimulation by sensory intruders is the sole cause for the steep rise in all forms of cancer in our time. Moods can be preparers of cancerous tumours. To begin with, they occur in the realm of the soul; steadily they sink down into the physical realm and settle on special, predisposed sites. Such places are the stomach when over-stimulated by artificial foodstuffs, the bronchi and bronchioli when over-stimulated by nicotine and its derivatives, and the skin when over-stimulated by the dust and fumes of the big cities.

Ill moods occur when cancer-like impressions penetrate our soul. After some time, good and bad moods no longer help to combat the army of intruders. They enter the realm of the body and turn into tumours. Today, every fifth person dies of cancer. The cause is the inability of the soul to digest the 'hidden persuaders' of modern life.

The four temperaments

Goethe, the great poet and philosopher, described the phenomenon of colour as the deeds and the sufferings — the active and
passive conditions — of light. He was of the opinion that
colours occur as the result of a constant interplay between light
and darkness. The red, orange and yellow side of the spectrum
is the victory of light over shadow; the green, blue and purple
side shows the defeat of light and the triumph of darkness. This
dynamic interpretation of the colour-phenomena will be of help
for an understanding of the human temperaments.

We have already described temperament as 'the dispositional mood of the individual' and said that it is 'the inborn
reactivity and sensibility of a person towards the world'. We
bring our temperamental colouring with us and do not acquire
it later in the course of childhood and youth. In our early
years, however, our actual temperament is superseded by
another temperamental colour which gradually wears off. By
the end of the second decade, the lasting temperament reveals
itself clearly. At about the twentieth year, the temperament-
formation is concluded and from then onwards, a person carries his temperament unchanged with him until the end of his
life.

Is it possible to describe or to define the nature of temperament? We have already mentioned that with a few exceptions,
modern psychologists do not regard the temperaments as psychic entities. Instead they speak of character or personality traits
or psychosomatic conditions.

Another group of psychologists who have tried to analyse
the constitutional differences in people have come to some
far-reaching conclusions. Kretschmer (1929) spoke of three
different types: the asthenic, athletic and pyknic forms of
man, which show very definite physical characteristics. Each
one of these three also displays special psychological traits and
these Kretschmer calls temperaments. A large chapter in his
book deals with temperaments, though he has great difficulties in stating what he really means when he uses this word.
He says: 'The temperaments are those parts of the mind

which (probably by means of the humours) are correlated to the physical constitution. The temperaments — either retarding or accelerating — influence the "psychic functions"; they give the colours to our feelings.' Here we meet a description rather similar to Gruhle's definition of temperament already quoted.

The widest possible application of this term is made by Sheldon. He calls his book *The Varieties of Temperament* (1942) and adds as a subtitle: 'A psychology of constitutional differences.' In his very precise investigations he comes to conclusions similar to those of Kretschmer. He also found three constitutional types and — although he names them in a different way — they correspond to Kretschmer's forms. Sheldon calls the constitutional make-up of a person his temperament, physically as well as psychologically. To him character traits are identical with the temperament. The whole personality is the expression of temperament.

Allport, on the other hand, says that 'temperament comprises the characteristics of an individual's emotional life, the subject's degree of emotionality, the sthenic or asthenic direction of his emotions and his general or more specific emotional thresholds (for fear, anger, etc.)' (Quoted by McKellar 1952, 266).

From these few quotations, it can clearly be seen that so far no common and generally accepted idea of temperament as a mental and physical quality exists. What is especially absent is the spectrum of the four temperaments. Those authors who describe the different temperamental forms include almost the whole character and personality (Sheldon and Kretschmer). The others see temperament as a general quality which makes the psychic motor run quickly or slowly, thus having its influence on the mental make-up of a person (Allport and Gruhle).

Rudolf Steiner speaks rather differently about the temperaments ([1919 Aug 21] 1977, 1967). He refers to the four distinct forms of temperament which Hippocrates and Aristotle recognized and described and he tries to give some meaning to these four types. In a seminar on education he called the two qualities which build up the temperament 'irritability and strength'. Accordingly, he described the four forms as follows:

> Melancholic — great strength and little irritability
> Choleric — great strength and great irritability
> Sanguine — little strength and great irritability
> Phlegmatic — little strength and little irritability

We can now ask what Rudolf Steiner means when he uses the words 'strength' and 'irritability' in this context. 'Strength' points to power and force; 'irritability' to a greater or lesser degree of sensitivity. 'Strength' in this connection means the living and enduring strength of a person. 'Irritability' is his capability of reacting; whether he is slow or quick in grasping a situation or impression and in making use of them. A sanguine person will be very sensitive to any new impression. He will grasp it quickly but will equally quickly turn to something else which may distract him from the former interest. A choleric person has the same strong irritability but is also equally great in strength. Such an individual will keep his interest in one thing for a considerable period and will not leave it before he has achieved an understanding for it and has mastered it.

A phlegmatic person is slow in reaction and weak in strength. He is easily influenced by his environment because he has little initiative of his own.

The most peculiar temperament is the melancholic. With little irritability but with great strength, it makes the individual hold fast to the chosen subject. Melancholic people will indulge in special ideas and easily get fixed to them. Among fanatics and specialists there are many with a melancholic temperament.

These few descriptions make it quite obvious that the different blendings between irritability and strength make up the four types of temperament. It is apparent that 'strength' is related to the power of will, and 'irritability' to the sphere of the senses. The sensory awareness of a person and his ability to recognize and to judge is the source of his irritability; it is connected to the realm of thinking. Thus in each of the four temperaments the power of will and the sphere of thinking are mixed. These two elements determine the whole realm of temperament.

In one of his lectures, Rudolf Steiner referred to these two elements of the soul, and after extensive deliberations he came to the following conclusion ([1920 Dec 5] 1980, 1935): 'Light is of the same nature as thinking, and darkness is of the same nature as willing' (*Das Licht ist gedanklicher Natur, die Finsternis ist willensartiger Natur*). If we remember how Goethe described colour as the result of the interplay between light and darkness, we now discover that a similar phenomenon occurs in the human soul; the radiating light of thinking in interplay with the darkness of willing creates the colour of the temperaments. Outside are the colours, inside the spectrum of our temperaments.

It would be wrong to think that any individual is determined by one temperament only. Everybody harbours all four temperaments in his whole personality; but one of the four is more pronounced than the rest. When we arrange the four main types in a circle, we see the following order:

Choleric

Melancholic   *Sanguine*

Phlegmatic

A *choleric* individual will always show certain melancholic and sanguine tendencies. The phlegmatic temperament, however, will in him be hardly recognizable. The choleric male (such as Beethoven, Napoleon and many others) will tend more to the melancholic side; the choleric female more to the sanguine.

A *melancholic* person has symptoms of phlegmatic as well as of choleric traits, but he will never show the slightest indication of a sanguine attitude. Everything in him will bear the mark of darkness and will, with little irritability.

The *phlegmatic* may display some melancholic as well as sanguine qualities. His choleric temperament is completely hidden and will hardly show forth. Here it is more the male who will have sanguine tendencies and the female who presents melancholic traits.

The *sanguine* temperament has a choleric masculine side and a phlegmatic feminine quality. It will never exhibit melancholic tendencies.

We now begin to understand the peculiar order of the four temperaments. It is a fact that two are always polar opposites and thus exclude one another. The phlegmatic individual rarely shows signs of a choleric temperament and similarly, the sanguine and melancholic are incompatible. Each temperament has however, two companions which vary in strength and appearance. Thus the variety of blending is manifold.

As the temperaments are influenced and moulded by many other qualities of the individual, two similar temperamental traits will hardly ever be found. Each person has his special temperament which is like the robe of his individuality. This garment is woven by the warp of 'strength' and the woof of 'irritability'. It is we ourselves who are the weavers of this temperamental material; we give it the special texture, the personal colour and the individual cut.

It is not always easy to recognize the temperament of a person because the three temperaments are often closely mixed and the dominant one loses its outstanding colour. It is, therefore, sometimes necessary to look for the temperament which is *not* present. If the melancholic quality is completely missing, the polar temperament, the sanguine, will be the main one. This diagnostic key is often of great help.

Another important symptom is the relation of the various temperaments to time. A melancholic person is deeply bound up with past experiences. He will always contemplate past happenings and turn them over and over again in his mind. He has great difficulty in forgetting what was done to him; his whole attitude is turned to times gone by.

The choleric person can easily forget. He does not like to repeat himself or to turn to experiences which have passed. He seeks for activity, he wants to oppose, to attack and to undertake new tasks. His face is turned to the future.

Both the phlegmatic and the sanguine individual are connected to the present. The immediate impressions are followed by the quickly and eagerly changing attitude of the sanguine temperament. The phlegmatic person likes to indulge in the present and does not care too much about either the past or the future. These two temperaments are children of the present

Mood and temperament in man and animal

We have come to a first description of the vast subject of mood and temperament in man. A short but necessary remark must be added about mood and temperament in the life of animals. Have these two qualities a similar standing in animals and man? Are we altogether justified in speaking of various moods and different temperaments when we refer to animal behaviour?

The modern science of ethology — which studies the behaviour of different groups of animals under normal conditions — has brought to light an enormous number of new facts. We have learned to regard the life of animals from a new point of view which has revealed entirely unknown sides. Each individual animal according to its species, its age, its environment, shows a special set of functions. It displays a very marked 'inner' life with a great variety of mental qualities far beyond the range of instincts.

The reactive behaviour of higher animals is a rather individual one and shows different traits even in the same species. The individual moods vary considerably and reactions, drives and motivations are differentiated accordingly.

Portmann devotes a whole chapter to the phenomena of mood in one of his principal books (1953). He sees in mood one of the prime movers in the behaviour of animals. He states very clearly: 'Mood is no longer a distortion or corruption of a "normal" or, so to speak, neutral condition. Mood is in itself in its different forms a changing "normality". A neutral animal does not exist; the living being is always in one or another form of mood whether it appears — seen from the outside — to be active or at rest.'

These few remarks and the many examples which Portmann describes make it obvious that moods play a much bigger part in animals than they do in man. Animals are not only permeated by their moods; they have little possibility to reflect on them and to change them. Moods in animals often motivate their actions and influence their performances deeply. American animal psychology describes mood as the 'central motivating state' (Buytendijk 1958). Motivation and mood are in animals closely related and we could even say that they depend on each other. Moods in animals create the motives of their actions, and the ways of action work back on the moods and alter them.

There are three special forms of mood in animals: the anxious, the aggressive and the erotic. This range goes through almost all the classes of animals and differentiates into more refined and subtle forms in mammals and birds. Nevertheless, there is a basic pattern of moods in the whole kingdom of animals.

On the other hand, the temperament in animals is no longer an individual matter; single animals have no distinct temperaments. It is much more the whole group or species which gives the temperamental colour common to each one of their individuals. The sanguine nature of the deer is different from the phlegmatic nature of the sheep. The cat-family is rather choleric in each of its members and so are many other species as far as we can judge. 'The cat among the pigeons' and the 'pike in the carp pond' are expressions suggesting temperamental contrasts in different species.

The family of the rodents is throughout rather sanguine. All their members are permeated by quick, restless and never-ceasing activity. They breed and eat much quicker than any other species. Whether mouse or rat, rabbit or squirrel — their temperament is the same.

Here we are forced to consider the fundamental difference between man and animal. The temperament reveals the fact that the individual in man corresponds to the species in the animal, where the whole family, not the single member, is responsible for the particular temperament.

The moods in animals motivate their actions; they will, however, be formed by the temperamental make-up of the family. The animal is bound and chained to the type of behaviour of its species. It is imprisoned in its outer and inner environment. Man is not. He is free to reflect on his moods and thereby to change them. He can recognize his temperamental traits and act accordingly. He can make the whole world his home.

Synopsis

A new realm of the soul has now appeared before our inner eye. Both mood and temperament revealed their true existence; they are the children of light and darkness. But how different is their being! How diverse their nature!

Light and darkness give the tension and the tone to our soul; thus our moods are created. The soul is like a subtle instrument in the hands of light and in the grip of darkness. These two elements tune the strings of our inner lyre to make it resound in a major or minor key. If the light is strong, we sing in sharps; if darkness prevails, we sing in flats. The strings of our soul are the handmaid of these two great powers which permeate the cosmic space.

The temperaments are the garment of our ego. This robe is woven by willing and thinking, the offspring of darkness and light. Darkness metamorphosed becomes volition; light metamorphosed changes into the power of thought. On the loom of our personal destiny, the linen of our temperament is woven long before our birth. We cover our nakedness with the garment of the temperament which determines the inner rhythm of our soul.

Once upon a time, before all things were made, there was the immeasurable and all-prevailing power of 'time eternal'. In Persia it was called 'Zeruane Akarene'. The great initiate, Zarathustra, told his pupils that out of Zeruane Akarene there emanated the two opposing powers: Light and Darkness. He named them Ormuzd and Ahriman. These great and powerful beings created the world, and at the end of their pathway stand the other two — mood and temperament.

Every human soul is still the battlefield of the powers of light and darkness. Today we no longer experience them in the disguise of Ormuzd and Ahriman. We behold them in a new metamorphosis: Michael and the Dragon appear before us and call on us to fight for the light and to overcome the darkness within and without.

We are called upon to change our misery and irritation into the light of clear thinking, and to accept in humility the dark threads which destiny has woven into the robe of our temperament.

Images now appear. The soul begins to speak of herself, to name herself, to describe her being. The soul sings the word of light and darkness and speaks the name of her makers who clothed her to walk with strength and uprightness.

Chapter 6

The Twelve Senses

The twelve senses of man

Modern psychology has the greatest difficulty in discovering the reality of the living soul. Mental and emotional facts are described and attributed to physical sources. The central nervous system, especially brain and spinal cord, is held responsible for the production of mental energy. Nobody knows what this 'energy' in fact is, but the concept of it gives the possibility to describe by name something which would otherwise not be explainable.

Why is it that the reality of the soul is so completely veiled from real experience? Every human being experiences daily his emotions and longings, his moods and feelings, his thoughts and volitions. Yet — the psychologist draws back from the simple statement: the soul is and exists.

There is no simple answer to this question because psychologists are human beings too, and have the same inner conflicts and the same ways of deceiving themselves as anyone else. Some of them are agnostics and unable to acknowledge a power for which they have no place in their world-concept. Others would like to admit the truth of the soul's existence but fail to believe in their own experiences. For the soul is evasive; it can neither be seen nor heard; it cannot be touched or measured. Its existence, therefore, is denied or questioned.

The reason lies in the soul itself. Its substance and being are so tender and impressionable that they disappear under the stress and strain of the impact which the senses convey to the soul. During the last century, the rising tension of human existence has grown to such an extent that the soul stands beneath a

constant hammering of sensory impressions which flow cease-
lessly through eyes and ears, through skin and other perceptual
organs. Under this powerful demand the soul itself seems to
disappear and become little more than a mirror for outer experiences. The life of the soul is drowned in the turmoil of colours
and sounds, of noise and moving pictures.

Is it any wonder that modern psychology denies the existence
of a mirror which is unrecognizable through the number of
images it reflects? A superficial observation of one's own experiences will justify this remark. What do we meet when we
observe the flow of our mental life? There are first and foremost
the sense-impressions which fill our consciousness. The world
around us is seen and heard, touched, smelled and tasted. We
experience warmth and cold, inside as well as outside our body.
We feel how cold surroundings can make us shiver and a hot one
makes us perspire. To shiver and to sweat are sensory experiences
as well, though different in nature from seeing and hearing.

In fact there are two different types of sensory experiences.
The one reveals to us the form and nature of the surrounding
world. We smell and taste its substance; we see the colour and
shape and spatial relation of all things around. We also feel their
temperature and experience their surface and its peculiarities.
By touching it we sense whether it consists of stone, wool or
metal.

The other group of sensory experiences gives to us a direct
impression of the condition of our body. We feel, though in a
vague and dull way, the inner surface of our skin. We have a similarly vague impression of our well-being. We sense exactly the
position of our limbs to each other and to the trunk as a whole,
because we know exactly whether we have an arm stretched out
or bent, or whether our hands are open or clenched. We are
continually accompanied by such experiences and feel either
poised or relaxed.

We are thus filled in our soul with the impression of the
world around us and of another world which we learn to recognize as our own body. It takes the child a considerable time to
distinguish between these two realms of experiences, and not
before the toddler has learned to stand upright and to take his

first steps is he able to differentiate between the one and the other. The uprightness of man draws a veil between the environment and his body.

Yet — the body remains to some extent part of the world. We inhale and exhale the air of our surroundings; at one moment it is outside our body and in the next moment it is part of it. We feel the temperature of our surroundings as warmth, which permeates our body and is radiated back into the outside. The life of the body depends on the condition of the air, the temperature, the available food and drink. Thus we are part of the world around us.

But we distinguish our body as different from all other bodies because a complicated and manifold system of sensory impressions makes this body to be our own. No other body is in this special form related to ourselves. Rudolf Steiner described four sensory systems which are responsible for conveying to our soul the constant signals of its own body.

1. *The sense of touch* — gives to the soul the dull experience of the boundaries of the body.
2. *The sense of life* — relates to the soul the well-being of the body.
3. *The sense of movement* — conveys to the soul the position of the parts of the body to one another.
4. *The sense of balance* — imparts to the soul the position of the body in regard to the surrounding space. Whether it is upright or horizontal is experienced by means of this sense.

These four senses which we may call the 'lower' or 'bodily' senses convey to us the constant awareness of our physical nature.

Four further senses are turned towards the surrounding world:

5. *The sense of smell* — conveys to us the individual odour of each substance. It reveals something of its own being or make-up; we 'smell' the nature of a substance.

6. *The sense of taste* — gives us an impression of the
   constitution of a particular substance. Whether it is sour
   or mild, bitter or sweet, salty or soft. Thus the
   'temperament of a substance' is revealed.
7. *The sense of sight* — displays the space and its contents
   around us. It pours the abundance of colours upon us; it
   makes us see the form and shape of all things and their
   relation to one another.
8. *The sense of warmth* — relates to us the temperature of the
   surrounding world. Whether hot or cold, temperate or
   stinging, we feel it by this special sense. It is particularly
   close to our own body and unites it with the
   environment.

The senses of smell, taste and sight distinguish very clearly
between the surrounding world and our own bodily nature.
These three senses convey to us the experience of the substance,
that is, the 'body' of the world around us. By the time we consider the sense of warmth the distinction is already blurred and
'within' and 'without' are not always clearly defined. We know,
for example, that it depends upon the temperature of our own
body whether tepid water is experienced as warm or cool. If we
have cold hands, the water feels warm; if we have warm hands,
it feels cool. It is, therefore, the interplay between the warmth of
our body and the warmth outside us which gives us the sensory
impression.

The innumerable data of these eight senses fill our soul to
constant capacity. Our mind is engaged in sorting them out, in
ordering them and in uniting them again in a new way.

These countless impressions, however, are permeated by yet
another vast realm of sensory experience: by the onrush of
noise, sound and tone. The sense of hearing is as manifold and
in itself as differentiated as all other senses together. It can only
be compared to the sense of sight when we consider the number
and variety of impressions we receive through the ear.

The eye keeps the world of light and colour, of space and
shape outside our body. The ear pours its experiences deep into
our system and makes our body and soul vibrate and shake

under its impact. That noise and sound often turn into unbearable threats for our soul is due to the special mode of hearing.

It is a new world that is opened up to us by the ear. It is neither our own body we experience nor is it the surrounding world's substance which is revealed. It is much more. The soul itself of things and beings begins to speak to us by means of sound and voice and tone. We perceive the mood and the feelings, the longing and the passions of men and beasts around us. The rushing wind and the creaking door, the sighing wood and the crackling fire, the moaning and groaning of animals, and the speech and song of people reveal the innermost nature of those who sound.

Their soul itself is sound and tone, is song and melody, and we listen from soul to soul when we hear. Whether it is the sound of nature or the speech of men; whether it is the murmur of water or the tone of a flute; it is soul that is revealed through sound.

Sound is the all-embracing, all-pervading expression of the individual as well as the universal soul. Thus the ear does not reveal the nature of substance as do the senses of smell, taste, sight and warmth. Sound reveals what is behind the substance, that which permeates the substance with mind and consciousness, with feeling and willing.

By means of sound and tone, man is able to transform his voice into speech. And it is speech that gives us the possibility of understanding the thoughts of another person who speaks the same language as we do. In this way, the material of sound, noise and tone is pieced together to form words and sentences which are the external expression of our intelligence and our reason.

Rudolf Steiner has pointed out that beyond the sense of hearing we must distinguish three more senses: the sense of word, the sense of thought and the sense of ego, thus completing a circle of twelve senses. He calls these last senses the four highest senses.

9. *The sense of hearing* — opens up the world of the souls around us. Through sound and tone, through voice and noise the innermost nature of things and beings reveals itself.

10. *The sense of word* — gives us the immediate impression
    whether sound is noise or speech. By means of this sense
    we experience the nature of words and syllables, of
    vowels and consonants.
11. *The sense of thought* — conveys to us the meaning of a
    word, a sentence or a phrase. Through an immediate
    sense-experience, we understand the significance and the
    symbolic content of the spoken sound. The name reveals
    its true meaning through the sense of thought.
12. *The sense of ego* — is the capability of the soul to
    experience the immediate presence of another human
    individual. We do not conclude by the presence of a body
    or a voice or any other impression that behind it is a
    personality who is similar to our own person. We
    experience the other ego directly.

The sense of ego is the last of the twelve senses of man
which give us the experience of three different worlds:

The four lower senses convey to us the deeds and sufferings of
our own body.

The four higher senses reveal to us the nature of the surrounding world in so far as this world is built up by substance.

The four highest senses give us the possibility to penetrate
into the soul-sphere of our surroundings. We hear the sound
and the word of the souls around us and thus we understand
their thoughts, feelings and motives. The sense of ego opens up
the innermost presence of the other individuality.

Sound, music and the intentional faculty of the soul

The inner quality of sound and music is always filled with a
very special attribute. When we listen to a melody — be it in
minor or major — we experience it in such a way that it creates
a certain element of longing in our soul. The character of
every sound contains a special element of yearning. The song
of the birds is a true example of this statement. Never do birds
sing in order to confirm what they have achieved. Their

singing expresses their longing for something, their wishes and desires.

With the rising sun in the morning, they start to sing and to trill, to carol and to warble, and all their song is a longing to rise higher and higher with the sun. There lies the archetypal quality of all music. Whether the shepherd plays his flute or the huntsman his pipe, it is always longing they express.

Music can soothe as well as stimulate. It can relieve our tensions and incite our phlegm. It can wake us up and sing us to sleep. Music plays with our feelings and emotions, with our passions and drives. But music never gives a true satisfaction and finish. The most beautiful melody leaves us with a longing for more. Therefore every piece of music is composed in such a way that repetition becomes the basic element of its structure. Whether fugue or aria, sonata or variation — the main melody or theme is invariably repeated in different ways and in various modes.

When we listen to music we expect these recapitulations because they are asked for by the innermost nature of music itself. There is no music without this element of recapitulation, which in itself is rhythm. And not only in music, but in every sound, every noise and every tone the form of repetition is part of its being.

The endless repetition of the waves is the song of the sea; the gurgling of the running stream sings the rhythms of the brooks and rivers. The rolling wheel, the stamping hooves, the clinking of metal, the ringing of bells, the repeated cries of beasts — they all occur in rhythms which are the inherent form of sound.

Similar to sound and music outside are the rhythmical functions of some of our organs. The heart beats because it longs for more blood; the lung inhales because it yearns for more air and oxygen. These two rhythms are the central motor for our life on earth. It is our soul that longs for air and yearns for oxygen in order to sustain the body as its dwelling-place between birth and death.

The beat of the heart is the keynote of our life's melody. It accompanies us day and night. Around this keynote the constant repetition of inhaling and exhaling is played and in this twofold rhythm rests the human soul.

This fundamental rhythm is approximately 1 to 4; about four heart-beats accompany the act of a single breath. Usually we count 72 pulse-beats and 18 inhalings and exhalings within a minute.

The soul, being in itself sound and music, can only dwell in a realm which consists of rhythm and repetition. By means of the beating heart and the breathing chest the soul inhabits the house of the body. As soon as this rhythm stops, the soul must leave the body for another realm.

The soul, consisting of sound and music, bears within itself the element of constant longing. Through its very nature it is filled with endless wishes, desires and drives. They belong to the innermost substance of the soul. It is sound, and sound is longing, and longing asks for repetition and rhythm.

We should now remember how we described the intentional faculty of the human soul (pp.27–30). We based our description on the work of the great philosopher Franz Brentano who, towards the end of the last century, characterized this fundamental psychic quality. We came to the conclusion that the whole life of our soul had this intentional quality, and that our emotions, thoughts and volitions were hardly ever without an object.

It is only now possible to follow up this first indication one step further. For we begin to understand that the intentional element in our soul is sound and music. It constantly seeks after an object, it longs for a fulfilment. He said: 'No hearing without something that can be heard; no faith without something in which we believe; no hope without something to hope for', pointing out by such examples that there exists no aim without a goal and that therefore all intentional acts are looking for their aims and objects. What Brentano described characterizes the true nature of music and sound.

Thus we can state that the intentional qualities in our soul are in themselves sound and tone. Therefore they repeat themselves and never stop. The quality of our soul described by Brentano as intentional is the same which we experience by means of the sense of hearing as sound and noise, as tone and voice.

Rudolf Steiner devotes a whole chapter of his book *Riddles of the Soul* ([1917] 1970) to the subject of intentional qualities. He describes the circle of the twelve senses in the way we have already indicated. He points out that as human beings we 'never receive an impression of a thing or being around us through one sense only.' There are always at least two senses which in combining their impressions enable us to perceive the reality of an object. He says: 'The connection to one sense appears with special clarity in our conscious mind; the relation to the other sense remains more hidden.' And he describes how especially the four bodily senses are the more hidden ones whereas the four higher senses stand out in bright clarity.

A few examples will explain this statement. When following an object with our eye — a flying bird or a moving vehicle — it is not the sense of sight which is able to comprehend the act of moving. Endless theories have been suggested to explain this simple experience but none is able to comply with the facts. Because as long as we remain within the realm of the sense of sight, no explanation is possible. As soon as we introduce the sense of movement which — by means of the eyeball and its muscles — can follow the object in motion, we start to understand this process of perception. The sense of sight combines its efforts to see a moving object with the sense of movement. The latter is more hidden and we are not as immediately aware of it as we are of the sense of sight. It nevertheless plays an integral part in this perceptual function.

Another instance is the following: in trying to bring an object into the focus of our vision, the lens of the eye must adjust itself to the distance at which the object appears. This adjustment occurs in such a way that the lens, similar to a muscle, is either contracted or relaxed. But it is not the sense of sight which is responsible for this action. Here it is the sense of balance which directs the refractory movements of the lens.

A further example: whatever we eat we do not taste through the sense of taste alone. Because as soon as fluid or solid food touches the tongue, the palate and the inside of our cheeks, it is the sense of touch that combines with the sense of taste. But we also start to sip and chew and thereby arouse the sense of movement too. The salivary glands begin to secrete their fluid and immediately the sense of life begins to function. Thus in the simple act of eating, at least four different senses are involved. They mix and mingle and their complicated interplay creates the experiences of eating, tasting and enjoying a meal.

In the first two examples it was the sense of sight which provided the melody in the intentional part of vision. The sense of movement and the sense of balance played the accompaniment. In the last instance, it was a quartet of music; the sense of taste played the leading part, which was accompanied by three other instruments — the senses of movement, life and touch — accompanying the main melody.

These examples are an indication of the function of intentional qualities in relation to the work of the senses. The four bodily senses are in a much stronger way connected to the intentional qualities than the four higher senses. In smelling and tasting, seeing and in experiencing warmth and cold, the quality of intentionality is much more refined. We do not long and yearn for everything we see or taste.

The lower senses, however, are imbued with such longings because they are filled with intentional attributes. The dim impressions we gain by means of these senses are full of sentiments and longings.

When a voice calls, I immediately turn my head towards it; when I see a person who looks at me with a friendly smile, I smile back. In both these instances, it is neither the ear nor the eye which induce my reactions. When I hear a voice my own larynx moves in response as a kind of resonance and immediately the sense of movement is called up, joins with the sound and makes me turn my head.

Something similar happens in the second instance. Through a slight imitation, the smile of the other person is repeated in my own soul; the sense of movement takes it up and makes my muscles move and return the smile. The two intentional acts meet each other: the opening smile and the answering smile.

We meet here still another element which plays a great part in sound and music: the element of question and answer. Every animal which cries out expects a reply. A bird which begins to carol waits for another bird to return its song and answer it. Also when man sings, he hopes for a partner and the charm of a duet lies in this action of giving and taking.

To ask for a thing is a refined way of longing for it; to answer is a subtle form of establishing one kind of contact. In both activities the intentional qualities are the real motor. It is the sound and the music of the soul which act.

With the higher senses, which are more concerned with the perception of the surrounding world, the object plays a much bigger part than the longing for it. In smell and taste the intentional realm of the soul is still strongly engaged. In seeing and in the act of pure hearing, these qualities remain in the background. It is the object alone which matters and not its relation to ourselves. It is, however, very rarely that an object is only seen or only heard. When this happens we are not able to establish any kind of contact with such an image or sound.

In connection with the foregoing descriptions and deliberations, we can now see how deeply our emotional and sensual life permeates the structure of our senses. Each sense-impression is filled with some intentional activity and it is the intentional act of the soul which relates to us the sensory impressions. We feel at home in the world which is revealed by the senses; but this feeling 'at home' has its source in the musical power of our soul. The intentional qualities bind our soul to body and earth.

Light and the transcendent nature of the soul

Seeing and hearing are the two main senses whereby we meet the world around us. No other sense is equal to them in importance and quality. The immensity of the spatial universe is seen by the eyes. The voice of the soul, its longing and greatness is heard by the ears. Two different worlds are revealed by means of these two senses. Eye and ear in themselves are as different as the worlds they expose.

The physical organ of the sense of hearing is closely hidden in the depth of the temporal bone. The inner ear has completely withdrawn from the surface of the body and has found a shelter which is safe and sound.

The eye is just the opposite. It lies open in a fold of the skin. From there it looks into the world. Something naked, perhaps even shameless is its character. It has nothing to hide but everything to show.

The world we see reveals its surface; the realm we hear opens up its depth. This is why our ear is hidden and our eye displays its form on the surface. (The outer ear has very little to do with the perception of sound; it is more like a guardian which stands at the entrance leading to the hidden seat of the inner ear.)

The world which the eye shows to us is a universe of width, colour and form. It can be light or dark, dense or transparent, hazy or clear. An endless display of unending possibilities occurs in the sphere of the light. Yet the light itself in its true reality is never perceived by the eye. We see the deeds and the sufferings of the unseen light, for the colours are the active and passive expressions of its being. But light itself is never seen. It remains concealed behind the curtain of the objects of the world of space.

Sound, on the other hand, comes out into the foreground. It discloses itself and wants to be heard. The sound is never shy like the true light; as voice and as noise it is decidedly aggressive. As noise it violates our sacred self in its peaceful existence and knows no barrier at which it should stop.

The eye is revealed but the light is hidden. The ear is concealed but the sound is disclosed. Here the polarity of eye and ear is apparent, but there is also the polarity of light and sound. The open eye reveals the garment of the hidden light. The hidden ear hears the revealed sound and voice.

Where can we search for the real light that hides behind colour and form? Is it possible to find it? We remember that in Chapter 3, when dealing with the nature of pain, we already met the 'true' light. When we described the different forms of pain, we recognized them as 'an immense spectrum of colours' and said that pain was the general quality of all other specialized sensory impressions, a unifying force making the perception of all of them possible. And we identified this spectrum of pain with the light which lies behind all sense-perception. We discovered that pain is light.

It is the same light which gives to each one of our senses the possibility to perceive. It is the power whereby we are able to 'behold'; to behold a smell, a taste, a picture, a sound, a thing and a being. It is the ability of our soul to mirror the world around it; to mirror the impressions and to make them part of ourselves. When I behold a flower, it is for the time of seeing a part of myself; when I hear a melody it is for that moment almost identical with my own existence. This power of perception, of holding and beholding a thing as an impression in the realm of any one of the twelve senses is due to the true light, this unseen light, which lies behind every sense and is a primeval part of the soul.

Here we again meet the quality which we described in Chapter 2 as the transcendent nature of the soul, pointing out that it had to be clearly distinguished from the intentional nature.

This clear distinction is only now understandable. Having recognized the intentional qualities as sound and music, we now discover the transcendent faculty to be identical with the true light. This real light is the creator-power of all space and form outside our soul. Within the soul, it is the formative force whereby the images of our sense-impressions come into being. This light is the active painter, sculptor and architect of our percepts and concepts. They are the ever-renewed creation of the true light within our soul.

The activity which makes us look or smell, hear or taste is of intentional nature. The creation of the impression and the forming of concepts is due to the transcendent element. Thus the act of smelling is brought about by the intentional quality; the smell itself in all its various forms is due to the transcendent nature inherent in the soul.

This co-operation and interrelation of sound and light is the real background for the functioning senses. The active intentional force sounds forth and the transcendent quality draws or paints the actual impression and makes it last for a short while.

The higher we move in the sphere of the twelve senses, the nearer we come to the realm where the 'true' light prevails and becomes especially dominant. We have seen that in the region of the bodily senses the intentional forces are particularly strong. In the higher senses, the intentional quality and the transcendent element are in a kind of equilibrium. Especially in smell and taste is this balance established. In the sense of sight, the transcendent element far outweighs the intentional quality.

In the three highest senses — those of word, thought and ego — the real light is of an all-pervading power. Here it appears in its glory. Like the sun that rises in the morning mist gradually dispersing the clouds of the night, the light of the soul transcends the spheres of the highest senses and leaves the sound of the intentional quality behind in the depths of the other senses. Hardly any form of longing and yearning remains with the sense of word and the sense of thought. Their percepts are free of sensory qualities. No colour or sound, smell or taste enter there any longer. Here the pure forms of concepts and ideas are met with and they consist of light which is no longer tinged by another quality.

In the highest sense, the soul is permeated by the spirit of the higher self and this spirit has its abode in the region of the pure light. Here the soundless character of the word appears. Its silent being is the true name and this name bears in itself the element of 'knowing'. By the sense of the word, we behold the silent word in the garment of the voice. The sense of thought experiences the silent word in the form of the name; now the word is free of the cloak of sound and appears in its own transfiguration. We behold its countenance. And with the sense of ego, we meet the being itself; we encounter the self directly and not any more its name.

Word, name and self are revealed through the three highest senses. It is the 'pure' light, the foundation of the soul's transcendent nature, which makes this appearance possible. This light shines into the soul; but into it the spirit radiates its power. This power of the spirit is the force whereby we are endowed with the gift 'to know'. This gift is not inherent in the soul. The soul is able to remember; it has the power to create by means of its transcendent nature the images of percepts and ideas. 'To know', however, is much more than to behold. 'To know' is to understand, to recognize, to identify; it is the kingly power of man.

This great and divine gift is beyond the unseen light. It is the power of the spirit which dwells in the light but is not identical with it. It is the spirit within the 'true' light which gives to the soul the quality of knowing itself and of recognizing man, earth and universe.

Synopsis

Twelve is the number of our senses that convey to us the impressions of the three realms of existence. The four lower senses connect us with our bodily nature. Our soul is chained through the senses of touch, life, movement and balance to its earthly abode, the body. The four higher senses reveal the world around us. The eye is opened to the width of space, while smell, taste, and warmth permeate our body like messengers from outside. The four highest senses bring us the signs from the land of the spirit. In sound and music, we listen to the inner movements of the souls of men and beasts, of plants and elements. When sound changes into voice, the word appears and in the word the name reveals itself, and behind the name the being itself can be met.

Thus — from below to above — the spheres of all creation communicate with our soul. And the soul permeates each of the senses with sound and with light. These two powers are the tools of the divine creation within and without.

Sound and music permeate man as far as he is a son of this earth: a being of fear and shame, of anger and joy, of love and hate; a human being who suffers and endures, who wanders from birth to death, bearing the yoke of his destiny.

Light and colour, vision and knowledge lift man above his earthly existence; they open to him the celestial view of his former home. The light reminds the human soul that the house of the Father whom we have left is still up above and that we — as prodigal sons — should reach it again. 'To know' is the promise that was laid into our hands. It can be kindled, and as a flame of knowing, carried back to the land of its origin.

'To know' is the bread we bake from the grain that grows in the light of the spirit within our soul. Our creative thoughts are the ripening kernels which provide us with the bread of knowledge.

'To live' is the wine which ferments and matures through the enduring power of our destiny. The sound and music of our deeds and sufferings, the voice of our conscience and the tone of our reverent faith cause the wine to ripen in the wilderness of our life.

But Christ offered his blood and his body to christen the bread and the wine of man. Through this sacrifice we were given the means to eat and to drink the bread and the wine in his name and thereby to participate in his own being. 'To know' in his name is the aim of man on earth. With the bread and the wine, he is able to open the gate of the house which the twelve senses have built for his soul's abode on earth.

Through this gate we enter a new realm of existence; we set foot in the kingdom of God. There we meet the divine splendour of the true light in which dwells the Logos himself, from whom the power 'to know' emanates into man.

Images now appear. The soul begins to speak of itself, to name itself, to describe its being. The soul begins to understand that light and sound, the bread and wine of its life, are the sanctified tools of the spirit's existence.

Chapter 7

Consciousness

The problem of consciousness

The question 'what is consciousness?' is one of the most fundamental in the realm of the study of man. It is not only a question in the field of psychology; a long time ago, philosophers inquired into the nature of consciousness without being able to find an adequate answer, and modern anthropology has started to approach this question anew.

During the last and the present centuries, psychology has deliberately overlooked this problem. When William James spoke about the fact of consciousness, he described it as 'not more than just the stream of thought' or as the experience that 'thought goes on'. He even said that subjective consciousness 'is the name of nonentity and has no right to a place among first principles' (quoted by Martin 1949). In a later essay called 'Does Consciousness exist?' he altogether denied its factual being.

A few years later, Watson, the founder of the psychological school of 'behaviourism', emphatically declared: 'The time has come when psychology must discard all reference to consciousness and need no longer delude itself into making mental states the object of observation; its sole task is the prediction and control of behaviour; and introspection can form no part of its method.' (Quoted by Burt 1962).

This is a clear and concise statement. It proclaims the nonexistence of consciousness because it can be observed only by introspection. Introspection, however, being merely a means of subjective inquiry and not an objective tool in the hands of the scientist, should not therefore, according to this statement, be used by modern psychologists. It is, no doubt, a matter of opinion whether or not introspection is an appropriate mode of investigation. Nevertheless, consciousness is a fact and if it can only be got hold of by introspection, this method must be used to investigate it. Neither William James nor John Broadus Watson would have been able to deny consciousness and to excommunicate it from the field of psychology if they had not been conscious. Without consciousness such statements cannot be made.

In fact, no statements at all are possible without consciousness because the greater part of our daily mental life depends on consciousness. Every human being when he either gradually or suddenly wakes up in the morning enters a conscious condition. He becomes aware of the surrounding world; he recognizes his environment and gains consciousness of himself. To deny or discard this fundamental fact of human life and existence would mean to cut out the greater and perhaps most important part of the human mind. In spite of the fact that no one but myself can know anything about my conscious state of mind, the knowledge is, nevertheless, a reality. And it should be clear to us from the start of our inquiry that consciousness is a purely inner experience accessible only through self-observation.

It is 'I' who know I am conscious, but I can assume with a certain amount of justification that others are conscious too. The way they speak and behave, how they act and react gives me the certainty that they are as conscious as I am myself. Though the condition of consciousness is a subjective experience, it embraces all our other experiences. When I look into myself, I can do so because I am conscious. In this conscious sphere, I experience at the same time the surrounding world, the beings and things, my memories and my emotions, my drives and my words. Consciousness is the ark in which I live.

As soon as we begin to inquire into the problem of consciousness, we are faced with the undeniable fact that it is a purely subjective experience. When we turn to other things, we simply take it for granted that we meet them and investigate them in the state of consciousness. When we inquire into the nature of light or sound, or search for chemical structures or organic forms, we can only do so consciously. We accept the condition of consciousness as a matter of course without any further discussion. In a similar way, we accept the validity of thinking as long as we do not inquire into the nature of thinking itself.

There is a common factor which applies to the quality of thinking as well as to the fact of consciousness. Both are the mental basis for any form of inquiry, search or question into the nature of man and the universe. Rudolf Steiner has tried to clarify the connection between consciousness and the process of thinking ([1894] 1964, 34). He says:

> I have so far spoken of thinking without accounting for its vehicle, human consciousness. Most present-day philosophers would object that before there can be thinking, there must be consciousness. ... There is no thinking, they say, without consciousness. To this I must reply that in order to clarify the relation between thinking and consciousness, I must think about it. Hence I presuppose thinking.

From these few sentences it can be seen how intimate the relation between thinking and consciousness is. A few paragraphs later, Rudolf Steiner says: 'Thinking cannot, of course, come into being before consciousness.' And we may add: Though consciousness is like the mother of thinking in the evolution of man and the universe, it is only given to the son, the process of thinking, to understand and to know the mother — the sphere of consciousness.

Thus consciousness suddenly assumes the position of one of the prime movers of our whole existence. What would we be without consciousness? Could we have developed at all without carrying the seed of consciousness in us? We could even go one step further and ask: Is any living being thinkable without a certain amount of conscious experience? And when asking ourselves this question, we at once begin to realize that there must be various stages of consciousness and not only the one we usually mean when we use the word 'consciousness'. We then refer only to the common state of awareness we have when we are awake during the day. But during sleep when we dream — is this not a state of consciousness, too?

I mention these points already so that we can at once realize how manifold, how varied and how all-embracing consciousness is. It is not as William James imagined a 'nonentity'. It is one of the fundamentals of all existence. And consciousness is so common and is such a matter of fact that it is hardly possible to define it in an appropriate way. Many who speak about consciousness simply assume that everyone knows anyway what is meant when the word is used.

Sir Russel Brain, for instance, when addressing an international audience on 'Consciousness and the Brain' (1961) introduced his lecture with the following sentences:

> I shall begin by assuming that we all know broadly what is meant by consciousness. ... Thus, we say that to be conscious is to be aware of things, and the things may be objects outside ourselves, or our own memories, thoughts and feelings. Moreover, we consciously attend to things, and our attention can be attracted or distracted. Finally we consciously exercise our wills and act upon objects.

In these few sentences, an attempt is made to describe and circumscribe the field of consciousness. It is not a very helpful description because the noun 'consciousness' is thrown together with the adjective 'conscious'; the latter, however, has a very different meaning and expresses a direction. To be conscious means to be conscious of something, to be directed to something or somebody, whereas 'consciousness' is a realm of existence and not an active engagement of the individual himself. In previous chapters we described the intentional quality of the human soul; the adjective 'conscious' is intimately related to this quality.

To be consciously engaged with a thing is an activity of the mind; such an activity can only occur in the sphere of consciousness but it is something different. And this is the great problem of consciousness: that it is not an effort of the personality nor is it an active power of the mind. It is a realm — a sphere of existence — a field of experience in which everything happens of which we are conscious. The whole time-space of our life continually passes through the field of conscious awareness from morning to evening. But what happens to consciousness when we fall asleep?

The different forms of consciousness

In the Lumleian lectures of 1947, Purdon Martin (1949) tried to approach the problem of consciousness from the viewpoint of an experienced neurologist. He goes a considerable step beyond Russel Brain when trying to define the state of consciousness. He says: 'I use the word to mean a sense of awareness of self and environment, well knowing that this definition begs many questions.' Martin is well aware of the fact that the 'awareness of self' is one of the most important signs of our common consciousness. He then goes on to say: 'It is not merely that I am aware of myself as a person whose presence and activities are visible to the outside world, but also I have a feeling that "I" am aware, that I know that I am, and that I see and feel and act. This feeling (I, the knower) constitutes "the very self" as Hughlings Jackson put it.'

In the sphere of consciousness, I experience not only my environment but am also aware of my body which is integrated into the surrounding world and to which my self has a special relation. Besides, I am conscious of my mental experiences and have interlaced into all these mental and sensory data the firm knowledge that 'I, the knower' am the central point of awareness in the maze of events. This focal experience is the thread of Ariadne by which I am able to find my way through the labyrinth of the Minotaur which represents the web of experiences in the realm of consciousness.

Every evening when I go to sleep, this thread slips from my hands and is apparently lost. But every morning, miraculously and without my own doing, it slips back and I can hold on to it as I did the previous day. Is it justified to say that we lose our consciousness when we fall asleep? Or would it be more appropriate to state that we change from one form of consciousness into another? Is it possible to call sleep a form of consciousness? And if so, does such a statement not contradict the very meaning of the word?

In the course of this century, we have learned to speak a great deal of the 'unconscious'. Analytical psychology as well as active psycho-therapy have taught us that the realm of the unconscious is not just a sphere of void, a nonentity, but the very opposite. We know that there is continuous activity and that a great variety of mental forces are constantly at work in this sphere. Our unconscious is at times more active than our day-consciousness. It provides us with many problems but also with many solutions. And both, the conscious realm as well as the unconscious, work together; a constant interplay connects the one with the other.

Are we permitted to call the unconscious a sphere without consciousness? Would it not be much more appropriate to say that it is a realm with a different form of consciousness from our usual one? It is a sphere of unconsciousness, not because it has no consciousness but because it is usually not as apparent to the self as is the common realm of consciousness.

Is not the domain of sleep a similar sphere? Do we not bring back from it the experiences of dreams? Are not often special problems for which we were unable to find an answer during the day solved 'overnight'? Sleep is a state of unconsciousness; nevertheless, it contains a form of consciousness we have to look for.

In trying to understand the apparent difference between sleeping and waking, by ascribing to both conditions some kind of consciousness, we may be able to bring order into this puzzling field of existence. It would be wrong to simplify matters in stating that we are conscious when we are awake and unconscious when asleep. In saying this, we would dismiss, for instance, the whole world of dreams, for we are conscious when we dream. But again it is quite a different state of consciousness from the one of the day. We would also dismiss the many dim experiences we have when asleep; experiences which provide us every morning with moral values and decisive convictions to which we came during the night.

When Purdon Martin (1919) tries to find the different states of consciousness drawn from clinical experiences, he points to four categories:

> Allowing for marginal overlap, we can divide the states of consciousness in which we observe our patients into four groups:

(1) the normal condition in which the person is responsive and reacts to psychological stimuli and indicates by his behaviour that he has the same awareness of his environment as ourselves.

(2) sleep, a condition of inactivity from which he can be roused and resumes his normal state;

(3) a state of unconsciousness in which he appears to be deeply asleep but cannot be roused to normal consciousness; and

(4) a much less common state, or group of states, in which the patient is awake and active but gives evidence that he is not completely, if at all, aware of himself and his doings, and of which he has no recollection afterwards.

When we consider these four categories, we can exclude for our present deliberations the fourth state because it is a pathological one. It is in itself very complex and most interesting but is not one among the normal states of consciousness. Purdon Martin, on the other hand, does not include the condition of dreaming in his scheme. He simply says that 'dreaming is another alteration within the sleeping state'. It is not justified to mix up these two states of consciousness because our experiences when we are a-dream are different from those when we are asleep. We cannot under normal circumstances bring memories back from sleep, whereas we often remember our dreams and can refer to them.

We therefore suggest that under normal conditions, there are four different states of consciousness:

1. ordinary day-consciousness
2. consciousness of dreaming
3. consciousness of sleeping
4. consciousness of deep sleep

whereby we infer that there are no hard and fast borders between these four conditions but that gradual changes lead from the one into the other and back again.

We should further understand that it is not possible to go from state 1 into state 3 without passing through state 2. Dreams are the subtle bridge between sleeping and waking. In a similar way we pass through ordinary sleep before entering the condition of deep sleep.

Each one of the four states of consciousness contains the possibility of changing into a pathological condition. When for instance a person becomes so elated that he no longer has any regard for the realities of life but sees himself as the central motor of all existence, his consciousness is then much wider and clearer than the usual day-consciousness. We call this condition a mania or manic disorder. The opposite is a depression or depressive disorder when the realm of day-consciousness is narrowed down considerably and little remains but some self-awareness accompanied by deep melancholia. The state of sleep can also turn into pathological conditions. Some people for instance seem to awaken in the morning but still remain asleep for the consciousness of their own self. They still sleep and are unconscious,* yet they are awake in some realm of their existence. The condition of deep sleep can turn into the pathological state of coma, which may ultimately lead to death.

Thus we have found a spectrum of consciousness. From the light of day-consciousness it leads through the colourful world of dreams to the shadows of sleep and at last to the darkness of deep sleep and coma. The importance of our discussion lies in the knowledge that consciousness is not a simple realm but a widespread world of different grades of awareness. We therefore agree with the statement Hallowell Davies (1962) made when he said: 'Consciousness certainly is not all or one. It certainly can be graded. It goes all the way from coma at one extreme up through the dream level to drowsiness, to wakefulness, to watchfulness, to full activity and creative thinking, to hyperactivity and perhaps anxiety.'

---

* This condition corresponds to state 4 as described by Purdon Martin.

'Awakeness' and the dimensions of consciousness

'Awakeness' is not a proper English word; we shall nevertheless use it because it defines a condition which is opposite to the state of sleep. We have described consciousness as a condition of awareness that reaches from coma to wakeful activity; we now need a word to cover the state of ordinary day-consciousness. And as 'awakeness' was already used in a very interesting and important paper several years ago, we are justified in using it again.

The paper referred to was published in a Dutch philosophical magazine later reprinted in a collection of essays. Its title is 'Some Remarks about Awakeness'. The author, Straus, says (1960): 'For the noun forms corresponding to the verbs "sleeping" and "dreaming" there are no direct antonyms. Obviously, in practical life no need is felt for a special word to describe a mode of being that, in any case, is the indispensable condition for all description and conversation.' Thus, the word 'awakeness' was introduced.

When we compare the condition of awakeness to the state of consciousness while dreaming, we find that a fundamental difference exists between them. When I am awake, I can look back to my dreams and may sometimes be able to recall their content and interpret their meaning. On the other hand, when I am a-dream, I am usually completely given up to the dream-world; I am part and parcel of it. As soon as I start to reflect on the dream, I already begin to wake up. Straus therefore makes the very pertinent remark: 'We describe the dream, so to speak, from outside, but we cannot look at awakeness from outside. There is no further retreat possible. The understanding of awakeness must be intrinsic to awakeness itself.'

Here we meet an insight into the relation of the different states of consciousness which may help us further to understand the whole problem. If I can look at my dreams from outside when I am awake, would it not be thinkable that in a similar way I look at my sleep from outside when I am a-dream, so that the higher state of consciousness always includes the lower? During sleep, I consider the condition of deep sleep from the outside. During my dreams I am somehow aware of my sleep. And during awakeness I look back to my sleep as well as to deep sleep.

In the sphere of awakeness all the other forms of consciousness are included. But awakeness itself cannot as it were look from outside from a still higher state of consciousness down to its own condition. It can only behold itself from within. On the other hand, it can be conscious of its dreams, it can know something of its sleep and deep sleep. Thus, the four states of consciousness seem to be telescoped into one another.

Here a condition is revealed which we can compare to the patterns of spatial dimensions. The one-dimensional line is contained in the two-dimensional plane and the latter is included and enclosed in the three-dimensional space.

A being living in the one-dimensional space of a line would never be able to perceive more than the line. It could move backward and forward but would be bound to remain in the line. A being living in the dimensions of a plane would have the possibility of being aware of the lines but not of the surrounding three-dimensional space. And only the inhabitant of a three-dimensional extension can look onto planes and lines and points as well.

Is it possible to carry this comparison between the states of consciousness and the three spatial dimensions any further and relate them to each other? It is tempting to imagine that awakeness in the realm of consciousness might be compared to the three-dimensional space. To be a-dream would then correspond to the two-dimensional space of the plane and to be asleep would be parallel to the one-dimensional line. Does this comparison contain more than a grain of truth? Is it more than a correspondence of the laws of logic?

Straus comes to a fundamental insight in the above-mentioned paper, which he describes in the following way (1980):

> Awaking from sleep we are ready to get up. To arise
> means to rise against gravity. Experiencing in our
> corporeality, we find ourselves bound — but not chained
> — by heaviness; in our ponderosity we long for levity

and buoyancy. ... In opposition to the ground and to the
Other I experience myself and that which is most truly
mine, my body. Partial conquest of gravity, lifting us from
the ground, assures us of our monadic existence, gives us
freedom for action. ... Through our heaviness we are
confined to the Here; through our motility, able to
conquer gravity and to move, we are potentially Over-
There ... awake we are held within the cumbrous
continuum of the here and now where the pendulum has
to swing through the seconds and minutes, where
sequence implies consequence.

It is most important to discover with Straus that awakeness is
intimately bound up with the ability to move about and to conquer the forces of gravity. This, however, is only possible by
being master of our three-dimensional body. It is our physique
that enables us to move, to meet the 'Other' and to conquer the
space around us. Thus, awakeness and the conquest of space by
means of our motility are intimately and mysteriously related.

The infant who gains the ability to stand upright at the end
of the first year, not only conquers space by learning to negotiate
the forces of gravity. He has also learned to face the 'Other' and
thereby to experience himself as being different from the surrounding world. In this moment, the condition of awakeness
begins. Uprightness and awakeness are intimately related and
both are correlated to the three-dimensional space.

When we go to sleep, we surrender our uprightness and
entrust our body to the powers of gravity. The floor, bed or whatever we lie on sustains our weight. We do not lift it up by our own
uprightness. We sink down and lie flat on a plane. We change
from our position in the three-dimensional space into a posture
which is almost two-dimensional. And now we start to dream.
Straus, in following up his deliberations, states: 'In the waking
state we can communicate with ourselves and with others. The
dreamer is alone in his dream world. No one else can enter it, nor
can the dreamer leave it.' The dreamer though aware of himself is
more integrated into his experiences than the one who is awake.
The dreamer is helplessly involved in the dramatic happenings

around him. Image follows image and he, the dreamer, is himself one image among the others. Whenever he tries to escape, his attempt is bound to fail until he at last wakes up. When a-dream, he is quite unable to get out of his dream, he is confined in the two-dimensional sphere of his dream-consciousness. It is a plane full of images in which the dreamer moves. In this plane, beautiful worlds can be mirrored and heavenly or hellish phantasies can appear. But dreams are never more than a mirror-picture, a mirage, an image. It is the plane of the looking-glass in which the dream-experiences appear; they are reflected images but not three-dimensional realities.

When the bridge of dreams is crossed into the land of sleep, all pictures disappear. We move from the two-dimensioned space into the realm of one dimension. Our body becomes but a line and awareness is very limited. It is just enough to keep the small thread of contact with our surroundings alive, through which we can, if necessary, be roused. A kind of gate prevents the outer impressions from entering into the world of the sleeper. He is confined to the one-dimensional line of his body; but it is a line which reaches far out into the cosmic space in which the real being of the sleeper dwells.

In deep sleep or when coma has set in, the body is nothing any more but a dimensionless point. It is the eye of the needle through which we move every night to re-establish our self and our life. Our consciousness is then spread out over the whole world; it is a cosmic consciousness which, though it cannot be remembered, nevertheless restores our strength for the next period of awakeness.

The evolution of consciousness and the unconscious

The four states of consciousness which we described and related to one another are not independent entities. They form a kind of stairway with four steps, each leading up to the next. Rudolf Steiner interpreted the four forms of consciousness as steps in the evolution of mankind. He strongly emphasized this mental development in the course of human evolution and explained how differently the mind of ancient peoples worked compared to the mind of man today. He was at pains to point out that history will only be understood when we begin to realize that man's present consciousness is fundamentally different from the one of three or four thousand years ago.

He introduced again the view that most people were still endowed with clairvoyant abilities in ancient times and that the fundamental difference between sleeping and waking we experience today was by no means so relevant in former times. A few thousand years ago, men were not completely unconscious when asleep but experienced certain images with a dimmed consciousness and were able to carry these pictures back into the life of the day. On the other hand, their day consciousness was not so clear and comprehensive as is ours. The things of the outer world appeared as if they were veiled in colours without straight lines and clear-cut forms. Only gradually did day-consciousness develop and things become clearly visible.

Rudolf Steiner described four different states of consciousness and gave each one a special name. The 'awakeness' of today he characterised as *object-consciousness (Gegenstands-Bewusstsein)*. Prior to this condition mankind had an *image-consciousness (Bilder-Bewusstsein)*. In primeval times preceding this latter state, men had a *sleep-consciousness (Schlaf-Bewusstsein)* and in the far distant beginning of all existence there was a *trance-consciousness (Trance-Bewusstsein)*. These conditions of consciousness correspond very closely to the four states we have already described.

To let Rudolf Steiner state in his own words what he means, I quote some of his explanations ([1907 June 1] 1979, 1981):

> In the whole world everything is subject to the laws of evolution; our consciousness, too, has developed. The kind of consciousness man has today was not always there. Step by step it has become that which it is at present. We call this type of consciousness the object-consciousness or the waking day-consciousness. ... It is based on the fact that man directs his senses to the outer world and perceives objects. ... That which he perceives by means of his senses becomes the object of his

thoughts. With the help of reason he tries to comprehend
the various objects; out of the combined faculties of
sense-perception and comprehension, by means of
reason, our present-day consciousness is composed. This
type of consciousness was not always there. It developed;
and it will develop further so that man will rise into still
higher states of consciousness.

Rudolf Steiner distinguishes all in all seven states of consciousness of which the present object-consciousness is the
fourth; three more are still to develop in the course of the future
evolution of mankind. It is of great importance to know that the
day-consciousness of our time is not the final achievement of
the unfolding spirit of mankind; it is but a step which leads to
still higher forms of consciousness. Just as when we look back
on our dreams and behold them from outside, so in times to
come shall we be able to look back to our present consciousness.

A special insight into the nature of the four states of consciousness is given by Rudolf Steiner in the same lecture from
which we took the above quotations. There he states that 'in our
surroundings beings exist which have the state of trance-consciousness: the minerals. It is a consciousness which is dull but
all-knowing.' In a similar way the plants are endowed with
sleep-consciousness. 'They are continuously asleep.' All the
lower animals, especially those 'which cannot produce a voice
from within' have an image-consciousness similar to the one we
experience when are are a-dream. Only the more highly developed animals, such as birds and mammals, rise up to the object-
consciousness common to man.

To understand the relation between day-consciousness and
the states of consciousness working in the three kingdoms of
nature is of great value. Such a view widens the concept of consciousness and brings it into unison with the whole creation.
The resting stone, the growing plant and the sentient animal are
conscious beings; their states of consciousness are not even different from those of man when the whole width of the evolution of consciousness is taken into consideration. Man is one
with the whole of creation.

Going to sleep, he withdraws from object-consciousness into primeval states of evolution. He submerges, first into the world of dreams and then into the sphere of sleep. It is a regression into his past, a withdrawal to the very fountainhead of his becoming. He returns whence he came in order to acquire renewed strength to enable him to withstand the stress and strain of life in the sphere of day-consciousness.

In sleep and in dream, we live and act in a realm which C.G. Jung described as the 'collective unconscious'. To him this region is a storehouse of 'the complete content of all the experience which mankind has made in the realm of the psyche' (Jacobi 1957). It is the vast kingdom we enter when we go to sleep. There we meet the archetypes and archetypal images; it is the realm whence the mythological pictures and the figures of legends and fairy tales arise. In this world of spiritual realities, we are rejuvenated and re-conditioned for our daily work.

The usual idea of the unconscious, as a kind of junk-shop of the individual into which he throws the drives, wishes and emotions for which he has no momentary use, is complete nonsense. The unconscious is much more than this; to use the description of C.G. Jung 'the day-consciousness assumes a kind of central position and it has to suffer being surrounded and towered over from all sides by the unconscious psyche'. Into the sphere of the collective unconscious some of our drives and wishes go and are met by spiritual realities. Such meetings are projected in our dreams and sometimes we are able to understand the symbolic language of these images and unravel their meaning.

The unconscious realm appears to be comparatively dark because the object-consciousness has assumed a very specific brightness. This brilliant illumination of our day-experiences makes our dreams fade into twilight and our sleep disappear into sombre darkness. There remains, however, a good amount of dim light in the sphere of sleep; but we no longer have any power to behold it. We meet with the same phenomenon when, entering a fairly well-lit room, coming out of brilliant sunlight, we are almost blinded.

The present day-consciousness is not only brightly lit; it is also exceedingly limited and narrow. It is not more than a shaft of light around which reigns a huge sphere of complete darkness. Man had to give up the width but comparative dimness of the earlier stages of consciousness for the narrow but brightly lit space of his present object-consciousness. In this confined but well-illuminated cell, we experience the clarity of our thoughts and the certainty of our self. Its three-dimensional space, not too wide and not too deep, is well fitted for establishing our personality until we find our way from there to the next higher form of consciousness.

The nature of object-consciousness and the human soul

Thus the four different forms of consciousness are described and discussed. We discovered the developmental relationship between the main types of conscious experience. But now the question of the nature of consciousness has to be approached. What is consciousness and how does conscious experience arise at all? Is consciousness part of our memory? Or is it part of perception? Do we therefore need sense-organs to acquire conscious experiences? But behind these questions stands a much more general problem: to what extent is the soul connected to the sphere of consciousness? What part does it play in the different spheres of consciousness? Are soul and consciousness identical? These are all questions for which no easy answer can be found.

When through introspection we look into the realm of the soul, we especially experience the ever-changing life of our inner world. Our thinking flows along, carrying with it words and sentences, concepts and memories, like a brook which carries waves and fish, stones and debris. Feelings arise, wishes and desires appear and judgments are made. We are, except in special moments, quite unable to stop the flow of this river of mental entities. Out of nowhere it comes and into the unknown it goes; it is a constant and relentless stream. Is it not due to object-consciousness, to this narrow shaft of light, that this stream appears in our mind? Is not the mind itself the sphere of consciousness in which the life of the soul can be experienced?

Rudolf Steiner discussed the same problem in one of his fundamental lectures ([1910 Nov 4] 1980, 1971). He states: 'Consciousness is something other than the flowing stream of the life of our soul.' He also points out that concepts and ideas we acquired and which became part of our memory remain in the sphere of the soul, but we are by no means always conscious of them. They appear in our object-consciousness and quickly disappear again. They are present though not always available. And he then concludes: 'Consciousness illuminates only one part of our soul's life'. He then continues with the question: 'How does it happen that light is thrown on this flowing stream of concepts and ideas which are not in the field of consciousness but are thereby made visible in the sphere of memory?' As soon as we remember something, the mental picture of our memory enters the sphere of consciousness. It flows from the realm of the unconscious to the centrally placed sphere of the object-consciousness. The vast field of our unconscious is the source and vessel out of which the elements of our mental life appear as if in a constant stream. But where does the light come from through which the conscious part of this stream is made visible?

To explain this, Rudolf Steiner points to a most important facet in our soul. He says:

> We find among our emotions different kinds of feelings
> — longing, impatience, hope, doubt and also others such
> as fear, anxiety, etc. What do these emotions tell us?
> When we examine them we find one thing common to
> all of them: they refer to the future; they point to
> something which may occur and for which we long.

This indication is of the greatest importance for our question. Rudolf Steiner then continues and describes two streams which flow through our soul: one bearing our concepts, ideas and memories; the other carrying our longings, feelings and emotions. These two streams run in opposite directions. The stream of our memories comes from the past and flows towards the future. But the stream of our wishes and feelings stems from the future and flows towards the past.

Rudolf Steiner, pointing to the opposite flow of these two rivers, declares:

> You receive information on the riddle of consciousness if
> you learn to understand that the stream of desire, love
> and hate comes towards you out of the future and meets
> with the stream of concepts coming from the past and
> flowing into the future. At every moment you are in the
> meeting-ground of these two streams. If the present
> moment represents this encounter in our soul, you will
> be able to imagine that the two streams strike against one
> another; this happens in the field of our soul. *This clashing*
> *of the two streams is our consciousness.*

It is not an easy task to begin to understand this description. We suddenly have to realize that two rivers of time exist, the one flowing out of the future, the other springing from the past. We have to abandon the usual concept of time running only in one direction, from the past to the future. According to Rudolf Steiner, there are two such streams flowing in opposite directions. Both meet in the ground of our soul and there, where they meet, consciousness appears. We can only say that the clash between past and future creates the present and that this present in us appears in the form of consciousness. It is the object-consciousness to which we referred.

In ordinary life, we are quite unable to take hold of the present within consciousness, because as soon as we do so, it has already turned into the past. In spite of the constant disappearance of the present into the void of the past it nevertheless is present. In its fleeting presence, it creates the realm of conscious experience. It is as if the flow of time were stopped and turned into space. This space is the transitory present which immediately dissolves again into time. We must imagine it as a continuous process of becoming and dispersing, flowing and fading; it is an unceasing coming and going.

As in a film where one picture follows another it is the speed that creates the impression of continuous movement, so here it is the constant stoppage occurring through the clash of the two rivers of time that gives us the experience of living in a constant present. This impression of 'constant present' is the nature of object-consciousness. But it is almost a figment which we have to hold on to. It provides us with the constant realization of our self as well as of the world around us; we live in the belief that our whole life is centred in this small cell of consciousness. All around this narrow shaft of light, however, is the life and power of the soul. From there it works, creates and is a servant for everything we do and know.

We have become conscious of ourselves but in having achieved this, we subconsciously feel that we have lost a vast kingdom in order to gain the tiny cell of consciousness. This is the destiny of man on earth; he had to become a prodigal son who left his father's house to descend into poverty and need. But a seed can begin to grow in the narrow space of object-consciousness, and a new and greater consciousness will be born out of it.

Coming back to the image of the two rivers of time, we may ask how they work in the realm of image-consciousness. When we are a-dream, we hardly experience a state of the present. Everything is floating and moving without halt and standstill. We may therefore assume that the two streams, though present, do not clash into each other as they do in the realm of object-consciousness. They rather pass by one another and some of their side waves meet and mingle, through which the images of dreams are created. Memories from the past and hopes for the future play into one another. In this way the mirage of our dreams is painted.

During sleep-consciousness, the two streams of time are completely separated. Our brain still mirrors the flow of concepts and memories coming from the past; but we are unable to take hold of them consciously. Our soul is given up to the other stream which comes out of the future and brings the events and experiences which lie ahead of us. In the morning, upon waking up, we continue with our thoughts from where we left them the evening before. But interwoven are some subtle forebodings or strong and driving wishes for the day to come. Thus the two rivers meet again.

No stream of concepts and memories flows through the consciousness of deep sleep. In this state of non-awareness, we long for the future but have lost our past. Our angel retains our former experiences and weighs them in his hands. He may give them back to us but he may also decide to keep them. Then is the moment at hand when we have to cross the threshold into another land; our existence changes from life on earth to life in the spirit.

Synopsis

In former times when the power of the mind in man was still endowed with the life of the spirit, our forefathers used to speak in mighty images but not in dry words. They described the past of the human race in pictures of four consecutive ages.

Hesiod, but other great seers too, spoke of these primeval times. First there was a 'Golden Age' when the first race of men lived with their gods; they were friends and companions. Everything was free of care and pain and there was no labour and need on earth. The whole world was like a garden. Eternal youth was given to all.

Following this race another appeared; the 'Silver Age' began. For a hundred years the son remained with the mother and she educated and guided him before he grew up. His manhood was short but strong; for the first time suffering started and many men turned into fools who denied their gods and refused to pay them their sacrificial tributes. This race was banished into the depths of the earth.

A third race of people was created; the 'Bronze Age' was inaugurated. It was a powerful but also a grim clan of men that now appeared. They had mighty hands and tremendous strength; they liked to fight and slay their opponents. Zeus, the divine father, decided to destroy them. He sent floods of rain down from heaven to earth. Rivers and brooks rose in a few days and covered the hills and mountains with a sea of water. The whole creation — plants, beasts and men — were drowned. But a single pair survived, the son of Prometheus — Deucalion — and his wife Pyrrha. Before the great flood had started,

Prometheus had advised them to build an ark and to enter it when the rain came. Thus they were saved. The ark landed on Mount Olympus and Deucalion sacrificed to Zeus. The god accepted him as the father of a new human race; the 'Iron Age' began. Some call this age the 'Kali Yuga'; it is an Indian word and means The 'Age of Darkness'.

These four ages are described in the form of images. They correspond to the four states of consciousness of which we have learned. We spoke of conditions of the human mind; our forefathers knew them too but gave them beautiful names and remembered the times gone by in fear and gratitude.

The ark of Deucalion and his wife Pyrrha is a true image for the state of our object-consciousness. Around are the waters of heaven and earth, just as our day-consciousness is surrounded by the ocean of our unconscious. In the lonely ark our self is preserved and present. The race of Deucalion can be called the generation of the ark. We are all sons of Deucalion, and we still live in the ark our fathers built to survive the flood of darkness. We carry mental pictures of the whole of creation within this ark.

But there arises a great question: How and when shall we be able to leave this ark of day-consciousness and regain the strong and safe mountains of the spirit?

The answer rests within ourselves. When we are willing and able to gain enough strength to call a halt to the two rivers of time which flow through our soul, when we can stop their continuity by the devotion of our heart and the clarity of our mind, then a space of the present will grow within us. In this new space a light will begin to shine which is called the 'Candle of the Spirit'. It shines into the darkness of the flood around us.

When many such lights radiate from the many arks of object-consciousness into the night of the unconscious, then the old images and symbols, the ancient archetypes and signs will be changed and transformed. The gate to a new age will be opened. The Child who was born on the first Christmas Night lights the 'Candle of the Spirit'. It is the love and humility, the poverty and compassion of the Child that makes this candle shine.

Images now appear. The soul begins to speak of itself, to name itself, to describe its own being. The soul understands that in the darkness of its existence, when it has forgotten its father's house and the land of the spirit, the Child appears to light the 'Candle of the Spirit'. This light will lead the soul back to the fountains whence spring the waters of life.

Chapter 8

Dreams

The land of dreams

The observant traveller coming from the north of Europe and passing over the Alps, is immediately taken by the complete change in the whole atmosphere of the landscape when he comes upon the shores of the Mediterranean. It is not only the brilliant light of the sun and the endlessly blue sky, not only the outdoor life of the people who spend most of their time in the streets and in the market places of their villages and towns. It is something much more subtle and significant. Everything seems to assume a different character and meaning; it is as if each house, each mountain, each tree and flower were to reveal its inmost sense and structure.

A woman riding on a donkey along a mountain path immediately engenders the image of the 'Flight into Egypt'. A peasant wife gathering some sheaves of grain in the fields at once assumes the figure of Ruth out of the Old Testament. A girl carrying a high pitcher on her shoulder and walking upright and straight from the spring to her house brings back the story of Isaac and Rebecca and their first meeting at the well.

This is one of the wonders of the South — that each event represents more than its outward appearance. It becomes representative for the inner meaning of many other similar events and happenings. Its symbolic character is much nearer and much more apparent. Everything is — to use the words of Goethe — *offenbares Geheimnis*, a revealed mystery.

The symbolic appearance of man in his environment is present in Italy and Greece, in Macedonia and Sicily. It is as if old mythologies were still valid and gods and heroes walked among the people. The traveller feels much nearer to the cradle of mankind and is imbued with the beauty and wonder of the old tales and stories.

Everyday life on the northern shores has almost extinguished such experiences. In Britain and Germany, the so-called realistic outlook of most men and women no longer leaves any space for symbolic appearances. The mythological and fairy-tale character of daily events has vanished. Plain life and plain speaking have taken their place. But they have not completely disappeared.

The language of mythology and the images of fairy-tales are still alive in the backwaters of the human soul. And every night when we go to sleep, they begin to speak to us and to weave the threads of their stories and pictures into our dreams. It is a language of symbols which the soul creates. A few of these stories we may remember when we wake up in the morning. It is usually the last remnant, the tail-end of the dream. Sometimes we can catch more than the tail and remember the whole vivid experience we had when a-dream.

Do we cross the Alps from north to south when we go to sleep? It is by no means the same, but a similar process; because we cross a threshold from one realm into another and on yonder side we are immediately in a different country. The laws and rules in the kingdoms of dreams are different from those which govern our waking life. It is a land that can be compared to the realm of fairy tales. Space is sometimes an obstacle but it is no hindrance. Time can be a threat but it may also completely disappear. Everything and everybody are exchangeable and in constant metamorphosis. My mother may appear as a young girl and my daughter as an old woman. My father may be at the same time my boss and my elder brother and all three are one. I can sit at a table with friends who have died long ago and whom I nevertheless regard as alive in their bodies. Inanimate things may begin to move, for instance, a huge bell suddenly starts to climb down the steeple and runs along the paths in the village. A flask begins to dance around my head, singing a mean melody with a dirty text.

The dreamer himself can be in several places at the same moment. He may stand on the banks of a river and see himself walking through the streets of a far-away town. He may climb a wall and on entering a room, find himself sitting there on a chair, both the sitter and the climber immediately merge. The dreamer may even become aware of the fact that he is dreaming and is thus split into the dreamer and the one who knows he is a-dream.

In a similar way the laws of nature's logic are removed in the land of dreams. The child may be the father of his mother and the son of his sister. A river bearing a boat flows up a mountain and spreads out into a lake on the mountain top.

It is quite impossible to enumerate the immense manifoldness of dream-experiences. They are thousandfold and every time new. Their sphere is the land of dreams, the border-region between waking consciousness and sleep. It is a kingdom of its own; it has its own laws, its own landscape and its own inhabitants. When we are dreaming, we enter this strange land and when we wake up again, we bring some faint memories back to the sphere of the day.

Our unconscious is not identical with the land of dreams. It is nearer to this land than our conscious mind, but it is not the same. Like our waking consciousness which is surrounded by the world of our senses, so is part of our unconscious surrounded by the land of dreams. It is a vast region; a realm which lies behind the sensory world. From this sphere stream the living forces of life and light, of sound and form. In this land, beings are at home which are unknown to modern man. But children are still able to play with fairies and brownies and with their unborn brothers and sisters. Those who have died live for a time in the land of dreams and sometimes have the chance to communicate with the dreamer.

Just as the sun illuminates the realm of day and the sphere of consciousness, so does the moon light up the kingdom of dreams. It is a land where sense-perception is subdued; memories arise and fantasy has its way. The active life of work is no longer valid. But other values appear. Human destiny assumes a different meaning and the hidden rivers of life begin to flow there.

Dreams are not fantasies or fancies. They are experiences similar to the experiences we have during he day. But instead of *here* we have them 'there', in the land where the moon rules and where symbols and signs speak their own language.

The interpretation of dreams

Before we describe the actual content of dreams, some indica-
tions ought to be given as to how an understanding of dreams
can be approached. The manifoldness of possible interpreta-
tions is so great that a short survey of their differences seems
necessary. There exist two opposite points of view. The one
regards dreams as mere figments and hardly worth mentioning
at all. A psychologist like William McDougall does not even find
it necessary to refer to the experience of dreams in his *Outline of
Psychology*. And in another well-known textbook on psychology
it is just enough to state (Woodworth & Marquis 1952):

> In sleep the brain activity sinks to a low level. Contact with
> the environment is mostly lost though some stimuli are
> perceived in a crude and bizarre way, as when the alarm
> clock is taken for an orchestra, or cold air on the feet for a
> wet path. More often a dream resembles a day-dream in
> being a train of thoughts and images which make a story,
> though usually without much plot and continuity. ...
> Some dreams are obviously wish-fulfilling. ...

Such biased and superficial ideas on the life of dreams are
still widely held.

On the other hand, there exists a large group of psychologists
and psychotherapists to whom dreams and their contents are of
the utmost importance. They hold the view that in dreams the
hidden life of the individual reveals itself in various forms and
ways. Thus the interpretation of dreams belongs to the main
tools the practising psychotherapist has to learn to use. Every
item in the dream — however insignificant it may appear at first
— can be a source of insight and may disclose a hidden story of
great importance. The dream is like an open image portraying
the wishes, desires and unfulfilled drives of the dreamer. This is
the other point of view.

Between these extremes, many intermediate views are held.
Today the science of dreams and dream-interpretation is so vast
that even the specialist is quite incapable of surveying the whole

subject, on which thousands of books and tens of thousands of articles have been published in the past fifty years.

It all began with Freud's book: *The Interpretation of Dreams (Traumdeutung)*. He wrote the manuscript during the years 1897–98 and its publication followed in November 1899. Jones, the biographer of Freud, writes (1953):

> By general consensus *The Interpretation of Dreams* was Freud's major work, the one by which his name will probably be longest remembered. Freud's own opinion would seem to have agreed with this judgment. As he wrote in his preface to the third English edition: 'Insight such as this falls to one's lot but once in a lifetime.'

It was indeed a piece of genuine research which Freud undertook there. Against the general opinion of his time which regarded dreams as a complete nonentity, he began to analyse the dreams of his neurotic patients very carefully. He compared this analysis with the content of his own dreams and the dreams of others. Thus he developed an entirely new and completely unforeseen theory of dreams. To Freud dreams were no figment, but psychological experiences of the greatest value. He discovered that almost every dream contains an element of wish-fulfilment. He even held the view that we dream only in order to achieve something otherwise denied to us in our waking life. Such wish-fulfilment is achieved in many different ways and forms. We may even dream in order to lull ourselves into continued sleep. A student, for instance, who did not want to rise in the morning dreamt that he had already attended some of his classes.

Freud distinguished between the so-called 'manifest dream-text' and the 'latent dream-content'. The dream-text is the actual dream we remember. The latent dream-content is the great panorama of psychic forces which produce the manifest text. Freud is not overly converned with this text; he ascribes to it only a kind of smoke-screen effect. The text tends rather to camouflage than to reveal. 'The remembered dream is by no means the essential thing; it is much more the distorted substitution which should help us — by recalling similar forms of impressions — to come near to the essential core of the dream, i.e. to bring the unconscious of the dream to consciousness.'

The discovery of the latent dream-content is one of the main endeavours of the psychotherapist. He is convinced that such a search inevitably leads to the source of most of the patient's neurotic and psychotic symptoms. Freud called the interpretation of dreams the 'via regia' (the royal path) to the unconscious regions of the soul.

There are several other factors which Freud called upon in order to interpret and analyse his patients' dreams. He speaks of the 'dream-work' which to him is the dynamic power of the psyche that turns the latent dream-content into the manifest dream-text. He also introduces a 'dream-censorship'; this is a force which stands at the gate between the latent dream-content and the actual dream and only permits certain symbols and images to emerge from the unconscious into the conscious sphere of the manifest text.

A kind of primitive dream-morphology begins to appear here. Freud took a decisive step by taking the matter of dreaming seriously. He began to investigate the content as well as the formation of single dreams. Thousands of psychologists followed up this 'via regia' and came to surprising results. Each one discovered some new aspects of the world of dreams and a great number of new facts were revealed.

Many of Freud's closer pupils left their master on account of their differences as to the interpretation of dreams: Rank, Jung and Steckel, to name but a few. Each of them discovered his own 'via regia' which he felt forced to follow up. Jung's approach led to his great discovery of archetypes; Steckel drew up a register of dream-symbols. Rank was among the first to find an intimate connection between the images which occur in dreams and those used in fairy-tales and mythologies.

A new world was suddenly laid open; it was soon visited and inspected by many. It became a kind of society-game to interpret one's dreams and to show that one was informed about the fundamentals of dream-symbols.

Today a much more sober view has begun to replace these fashionable tendencies. One begins to understand that dreams are likely to please the dreamer as well as the interpreter. A patient who is treated by a psychotherapist of the Jungian school usually produces dreams which contain a great number of archetypes and mandalas; whereas another patient who is under the care of a Freudian analyst will dream in such a way that many sexual symbols appear which then give satisfaction to the psychotherapist. Others who are fundamentally opposed to any kind of psycho-analysis will only dream of daily memories which are slightly, not basically distorted.

Hoche (1927), for instance, a strict opponent of all psycho-analysis made the observation that at the time when he was turning his attention to dreams, he began to dream much more frequently than before. And Leonhard (1951) makes the remark 'that at different times just those dreams appear much more often for which I developed a special interest'.

Not only are dreams evasive, but they are also pliable, to the dreamer's thoughts and desires and to his environment as well. Dreams like to please, to warn, to admonish, to frighten, to soothe. They can lift us up to the heights of beauty and wonder; but they can also let us sink into the depths of misery and fear. Dreams are difficult to hold fast, nor is it possible to ascribe to them a single task or meaning.

The land of dreams is a new and vast realm which is at least as manifold as are the spheres of our sensory world. The manifest dream-text is the result of the work of innumerable forces, influences and memories. It contains our sympathies and antipathies, our longings and our desires. But dreams are not only a result; they are a creation which starts its own life. Certain dreams can re-appear at special times and almost haunt their master. They can develop a form of conscience which keeps the dreamer aware of special traits in his character and doings. All these tendencies must be borne in mind when a right understanding of dreams and their world is sought for.

The content of dreams

There can be little doubt that a certain number of our daily experiences re-appear in our dreams. This is a commonly

accepted fact though it is not as simple as usually thought. The
way in which these experiences present themselves during a
dream is peculiar and interesting.

Rudolf Steiner drew our attention to the fact that we usually
dream about things which have passed by our day consciousness
unnoticed. For instance, we receive a letter and read its contents
very carefully. In our subconscious we may accompany the reading with either a slight sympathy or antipathy towards the handwriting. The following night we will not dream about the
contents of the letter but much more about the writer in connection with our pleasure in or aversion to his handwriting.
'Therefore it is so difficult to gain a real understanding for
dreams,' Rudolf Steiner says, 'because so many things appear in
them which remain outside our awareness during the day'
([1918 April 2] 1985). We receive hundreds and thousands of
impressions every day but only very few of them enter our consciousness. These unnoticed perceptions are, in spite of their
fleeting appearance, part of our experience and impress themselves on the deeper and subconscious layers of our soul. And
just these impressions rise at night and appear in our manifest
dreams. They comprise some of their main material. A number
of experiments, especially those of Pötzl (1917) have confirmed
this observation.

Leonhard later emphasised these findings and exemplified
them by many instances. Some of these examples may be
quoted (1951, 26f):

> After having met a child in the course of the day I dream
> in the following night about the whole family but
> without the child himself. The parents and the four
> siblings sit around a table but the child I saw on the
> previous day is missing in my dream ... After having had
> a very important telephone conversation during the day, I
> dream that I am called to the telephone. A nurse comes
> towards me and announces the call. I can see and
> recognize her very well. In the morning I suddenly
> remember that she is just the nurse I had not seen for a
> fortnight because she was on holiday. I had met all the

other nurses the previous day ... I observe a squirrel
during the day and am astonished at its lack of shyness. I
wonder whether cats hunt squirrels. The following night
I see a cat hunting a mouse in my dreams. I perceive the
cat rather vaguely but the mouse very distinctly.

Leonhard describes the image of the cat as the 'peripheral'
dream-picture and the mouse as the 'central' one. And it is very
interesting that as in the case of the other dreams the central
impression of the previous day is omitted and a substitute picture introduced. The squirrel is replaced by the mouse. The
leading thought, however, appears in the image of the cat hunting the mouse. Similarly the parents and siblings sit around the
table but the 'central' image, the child himself, is missing. The
nurse who was *not* seen replaces those who were noticed.

This is a fundamental observation which everyone can
repeat when he follows up his own dreams. Leonhard showed
that it takes from ten to thirty days before a central day experience is ready to appear as the content of a dream.

The different senses are rather unequally distributed in the
production of dream-material. There can again be no doubt that
our spatial observations provide most of the content of dreams.
We see a landscape, people, moving and changing objects. But it
is rarely the case that these images are accompanied by noise,
sound or music. We hardly ever hear the rushing wind or the
tinkling of a bell. We sometimes perceive a spoken word but this
is not often. Smell and taste, especially the first, almost never
appear in dreams. On the other hand, experiences of touch,
pressure, heat, cold, and so on, are very frequent.

The different sensory experiences are almost never integrated during a dream. They do not fuse as they do in our waking life. They are separate experiences and this separation and
lack of integration is one of the reasons for the unreality of our
dreams.

During the day, not only do we see an object but we can
touch it at the same time. This twofold experience gives us the
conviction of its reality. Touch, sound, noise, heat and cold give
us the foundation for the reality-experience in daily life.

Dreams are just images; they appear and disappear like fig-ments and rarely can we touch them or hear their sound or voice. Only in dreams which draw towards awakening are expe-riences of touch and sound in the foreground. Here, however, direct sense-perceptions are making their way into the realm of dreams. An alarm clock which begins to ring or the pressure of a wrinkled blanket which disturbs us interrupts our dreams.

Ewald (1929) assumes that optical dreams are connected with deep sleep whereas acoustical dreams are more frequent soon after going to sleep or shortly before waking up. I am almost certain that acoustical and tactile dream-experiences almost always have their source in direct sensory impressions. The same applies to experiences of smell and taste.

Another observation which can frequently be made is of great importance for an understanding of the dream-content. Dreams are usually colourless. Rarely can a specific colour be distinguished in connection with the images in a dream. The pictures are not even grey or black or white. They are simply colourless, like a dim landscape in a hazy and cloudy moonlit night. We may perceive the 'central' objects of the dream very sharply; but it is not the outline and form we see. It is much more the gesture of their shape and the figure of their mobility that impress us and make us recognize them.

Dreaming of stampeding horses, we behold much more their movement and the figures of their jumps and their running than the actual shape of their bodies. Seeing a snake drawing near, we experience the threat in its attitude and perhaps the split mouth, but neither colour nor proper form can be distinguished.

There are, however, dreams that have some outstanding colourings and Leonhard refers to them. He made the discovery that just those colours are repetitions of perceptions from the previous days. He reports on some convincing examples.

The greater the symbolic character grows in a dream, the more colourful will it become. We may even call this a rule for the composition of dream-material.

When we now try to connect these various observations and to draw some conclusions, we may state the following: Dreams are usually without any colour. They present themselves in the

form of pictorial impressions whereby a 'central' theme is surrounded by some 'peripheral' accessories. The 'peripheral'
images are usually connected with experiences of the previous
day which did not directly reach our active consciousness. The
'central' theme points to impressions received some time
before. Any other sensory impressions such as touch, sound,
warmth, and so on, are usually direct sensory experiences which
break through the threshold of sleep and lead to a change of
consciousness; we begin to wake up.

In considering these phenomena we can say that the content
of dreams is shy of any sensory qualities. It avoids colour, shape
and outline and appears much more like vague impressions than
objective images. Remembering the long span of time which
lasts between an optical impression and its re-appearance as a
dream-image we may even say that pictures which occur in
dreams do so after they are stripped of almost all their sensory
qualities.

When we dream of a colour (the white snow, a yellow
chicken, a green curtain) we either carry the colour from the
previous day right down into our dream, or old memories, laden
with special emotional ties, rise up. The colour from the previous day is still vivid in our perceptual experience and appears in
the dream like any other sensory impression. The emotionally-
tinged colour could no longer free itself from its strong bond
and arises, therefore, as a fixed sense-perception.

We now begin to understand that the content of dreams is
woven out of specific mental qualities. It is an experience without the qualities our senses can provide. In certain instances,
such qualities may attach themselves to the dream-material,
either by directly breaking through the threshold of sleep into
the sphere of the dream or by other means which are enforced
by emotional powers. The factual dream-content is, however,
free of the sensory quality.

This being the case, we should ask ourselves the next question: What kind of images and pictures appear in dreams? Are
they comparable to our memories, or even one and the same? If
not, what kind of stuff are they made of? Before we can tackle
this problem, we must turn to other facts of special significance.

The dimensions of dreams

Leonhard (1951, 76–78) is very puzzled when he tries to understand why the dreamer accepts without question the changing
objects during a dream. He says:

> One cannot refer to the loss of comparable facts if one
> takes a sled for a boat and a book for a bathing suit ...
> The dreamer knows very well what he wants. He wants
> to enter the boat; he wants to put on his bathing suit. He
> knows equally well what a boat looks like and what a
> bathing suit is for. But he is unaware that something else
> appears instead ... The dreamer who on the one hand is
> able to think sensibly is, nevertheless, quite unable to
> distinguish between a boat and a sled.

Leonhard refers here to two specific dreams in order to
demonstrate a very common dream-experience. The dream
offers quite different pictures from those we would have
expected to appear. A sled would without difficulty glide over
rocks and water, and a book can replace a bathing suit. As a
dreamer we would never question such exchanges.

We would equally well accept a person who quickly changes
into an animal and then into a child. Some figures in our dreams
may speak with the voice of an old friend, bear the face of one's
mother and have gestures of one's wife. Such transmutations are
fully acknowledged as though they were the most natural
things.

Leonhard is of the opinion that these phenomena are due
to the fact that 'the single dream-elements do not form an
organic connection but remain next to each other as independent units; they appear one after another alternately in the
dreamer's consciousness'. He describes this condition as 'the
narrowness of the dream-consciousness' which makes it
impossible for the dreamer to compare different experiences
with one another. 'For the momentary consciousness of the
dreamer, there exists simply that which is now and not that
which has just been.'

It does not seem that such an explanation can solve these problems. It may hold good for some dreams; in others, however, we follow up the whole trend of events which we can later remember. If it were as Leonhard thinks, we should never be able to recall a consecutive row of images with some meaning behind them.

As long as we expect things in a dream to happen as they do in our waking life, we naturally are confronted by many puzzles. But the state of consciousness in a dream is fundamentally different from the object-consciousness of the day. When we are a-dream, our limbs are motionless. Initiative and will are almost obliterated and the soul is in a condition of complete surrender. We accept the pictures that are given to us because we are unable to will and to want something else. We may be unhappy about something that occurs or even despise certain events or images. Our thoughts may be full of doubts and questions during a dream, but we are helpless and paralysed. A dreamer is always an observer, even when he moves. He is forced to do things in the way in which the dream makes him act.

The dreamer has hardly any recourse to his waking consciousness. He can take events and emotions, ideas and intentions from his daily life into the world of dreams. But when a-dream, the soul is unable to refer back to waking life. During the dream, only a one-way traffic is possible: from day-consciousness to dream-consciousness. The way back is not free until the dream has come to an end. Then the manifest dream-text rises into the object consciousness and we say: Last night I had a dream. But in the dream itself the road to consciousness is completely blocked. This is one of the fundamental dream-laws which so far has never been taken into consideration.

L.R. Müller (1948), for instance, describes a dream in which he discusses with his son the kind of study he should take up in the next few months. In waking up, he becomes painfully aware that his son was killed in action a few months before. The same author dreams of a lecture he gives to a medical audience. He speaks on 'Development and Treatment of Infectious Diseases'. Everything is very vividly experienced but 'only after waking up at 6.15 in the morning, do I realize that all these experiences do not refer to reality and were figments of a dream'. Müller was a neurologist and would never have read a paper on infectious diseases.

Such observations are common but not fully taken hold of. And what once upon a time, Chuang Tzu, the Chinese philosopher, said, no longer holds good for our time. He, waking up one morning, pondered: 'Last night I dream I was a butterfly. How do I now know whether I am a man who dreamt he was a butterfly, or a butterfly that dreams it is a man?' It may well be that such a question was justified two thousand years ago. Today we know very well the difference between dreaming and waking-life as long as we are not a-dream. When we dream, however, we are unable to refer back to our object-consciousness and have therefore no points of comparison. We are enshrined in the dream-world like a chrysalis imprisoned in its cocoon. This comparison goes even further because also like a chrysalis we are not a unified being in our dream. Just as the organs of the chrysalis fall apart and undergo partial or complete metamorphosis, so do our dream-experiences. Images come and go, change and return, and it is the dream itself that holds everything together.

Dream-consciousness is picture-consciousness. The pictures have no depth or three-dimensional quality. They are flat, extended only in width and length. A landscape is as flat as a room and resembles much more a mirror-image than an optical experience. People and things move in and out differently from the way in which they appear and disappear in the world of the senses. The dream is a stage without depth. The central theme of the dream is the focus, whereas the more peripheral events are hazy and indistinct. This arrangement confirms the fact that in a dream we have neither foreground nor background. A centre is surrounded by a periphery just as a focus is surrounded by a circle.

The two-dimensional dream-plane, though flat, need not be straight. It can be a curved plane with elevations, recesses and valleys which may convey the impression of a third dimension. But the sphere is a two-dimensional one and part of the image of our self is embedded in this flat space.

As soon as a dream draws to its close, it breaks open into the third dimension, a step which usually happens abruptly. It is like a bang, or a bump, or a fall. We open our eyes and are awake!

The realm of dreams is an entirely different space from the one of our waking life. Dreams do not occur 'within' us; they do not happen 'within' our body or 'within' our soul. It is the reverse. *We* occur within our dreams. It is I who am 'within' the events of the dream. The dream is not mine; it is much more the case that I, or part of myself, am also a part of my dream. We shall presently come back to this important conclusion.

Various types of dreams

Innumerable types of dreams exist. Even every single individual has his personal kind of dream. Each author who bases his investigations on the experience of his own dreams attains a rather narrow concept of the whole world of dreams. Jung has his own dream-experiences which differ completely from Freud's or Leonhard's. Each of these dreams, however, represents some common features which can be found in almost every dream.

Jung's dreams are filled with a world of symbols and archetypes. Freud's dreams represent complicated events full of intellectual absurdities and pictures. Leonhard's dreams are packed with memories and intentions which refer to daily life. Most of them hardly need to be interpreted. They are too simple and too much a matter of fact.

Aeppli (1960) distinguishes between the 'small' and the 'great' dreams. The small dream he calls an 'everyday dream'.

> All these dreams refer to the hither and thither, the ups and downs of our daily life. When one catches their meaning, one can just smile. These small dreams mirror the situations of the yesterday, of today and the morrow; they complete them with regard to matters which did not become fully conscious.

On the other end of the dream-scale, there are the 'great' dreams. Of those Aeppli says:

In the grand dreams which only occur rarely, the dreamer
meets with psychic contents of the greatest significance
and most impressive formation. After a short
introduction, everything disappears which may still be
reminiscent of personal experiences connected with the
events of the dreamer's daily life. The problems of the
day withdraw and the dream enters into a world filled
with an elementary experience of spirit and nature. The
great dream speaks exclusively the language of symbols
which are condensed from the fundamentals of human
existence ... The experience is often of incredible beauty,
reminding one of great poetry; sometimes the dream is
one of dreadful gloom, leading into the darkest chaos of
life. The dreamer may be led into the consuming light of
a mighty sun, into wondrous landscapes and to meetings
with people never seen before ...

These dreams announce important changes which will happen in the life of the dreamer. They mostly occur at the cross-
roads of our destiny.

Between the small and the great dreams there are the
'important' dreams, as Aeppli calls them. 'One receives indica-
tions from them and sees situations in a wider view. They contain a number of symbols and mythical motives; they lead into
archetypal situations but still use the language of daily life, taking the images based on the dreamer's common experiences.'

Here the general spectrum of dreams is laid out before us.
It is a scale which leads from the small dreams which usually
occur nightly, over the important dreams which are much
rarer, on to the few great dreams which happen only seldom in
life. When we compare the content of these dreams we see at
once that they draw their substance from two different
sources. The small dreams take their material from the experiences of daily life. The great dreams have a purely spiritual
character; their substance flows from the well of the spirit into
the womb of the dream. The important dreams draw their
content from both the world of the senses and the world of the
spirit.

With regard to their interpretation, we can say that small dreams need hardly any explanation, they are a conglomerate of drives, memories, intentions and emotions mixed with a few thoughts. The important dreams are those which need to be interpreted. With the help of signs and symbols, they try to explain the memories, events and intentions of the dreamer. Their interpretation and explanation can be of the greatest value.

The great dreams are beyond any interpretation. They speak for themselves. Just as a great piece of art should never be interpreted, so should one never interpret a grand dream. It is a gift from the spirit to the dreamer — like the angel who appears to Zacharias and announces the birth of John, or the Archangel Gabriel who spoke to Mary, or Daniel beholding the vision of the Cosmic Man. Such dreams are events; they accompany the dreamer throughout his life and he can continually draw strength and reassurance from them.

Other kinds of typical dreams exist. Everyone remembers the so-called 'waking-up dream'. We mentioned it before but it is significant because here, too, two different spheres penetrate the threshold of sleep. It is either an outer sensory stimulus — a knocking at the bedroom door, the waking noises around the sleeper, the ring of the alarm clock, and so on. But it can also be induced from another side: an inner sensory stimulus which is engendered by the dysfunction of organic processes. Cold feet, palpitation, pains in the stomach, flatulence, the bladder filled to capacity, toothache and many other such sources induce waking-up dreams. We imagine ourselves standing in icy water, or we experience the rushing heart as a hot oven which sets the room on fire. Such experiences, be they sensory ones or the result of organic dysfunctions are immediately transformed into an image. This is the language of the dream which is spoken in the world of image- or picture-consciousness. As soon as the pictures assume a threatening or dangerous quality, fear, shame or anxiety arise and tear the dreamer back into the land of three-dimensional space.

A special form of the waking-up dream is the so-called 'death-dream'. It only occurs with people who are seriously ill and are expected to die soon. Some of them recover and are able to recall their experiences. Aeppli describes one such dream and the most moving one is reported in the autobiography of C.G. Jung (1962). He tells of the most wondrous events he experiences, floating high up above the earth. In the midst of light and colours, clouds and beings, he has exceptional spiritual adventures.

'Great landscapes, eruptions of light through wild and dark gates appear', says Aeppli. 'Voices speak out of unseen depths; shining castles stand on mountains bathed in light; someone calls for a journey over river and sea.' Such are the last dreams a man can have. They build the bridge into the land of the spirit and help the soul at the gate of death to take the step from here to the yonder side of existence.

The death-dream assists the soul to remove the barriers of object-consciousness and break through to a higher state of awareness. After death we are able to look back on our life on earth just as we now look back to our dream-experiences.

The dream is one state of consciousness; we withdraw into it nightly. Our waking life is another form of consciousness common to us here on earth. Beyond lies a further state of consciousness which we can reach when we cross the gate of death.

The nature of dreams

Our attempts to collect some facts about dreams made it possible to see the whole problem in a new light. We regarded dreams as something real and found that they occur in a state of consciousness which is different from our waking-consciousness. Dreams are another form of existence though less real than our daily life.

We considered the relation between these two states of consciousness and found that we have no possibility to refer back to our day-experiences when we are a-dream; they are completely obliterated and appear again only after we have awakened. We described this phenomenon as one of the fundamental rules for an understanding of dreams.

Other questions still remained open. We hesitated to say what we actually behold when we observe the various dream-images.

From where do they come? Are they memories that arise? As compared to usual memory-pictures, they appear in a different form. They are less distinct, miss their colouring and are altogether of a different quality. They are hazy, strange and in continuous metamorphosis. And they lack one of the basic attributes of all memories: the experience of the *déjà vu*. It is the feeling which refers back to the perception from which the memory developed.

As soon as a memory arises in our mind, we immediately recognize it as a 'memory'. We remember the first and the following instances which produced this special memory. In our dreams, however, the *déjà-vu* phenomenon does not occur. The dream-images are experiences of the present and very seldom do we have a feeling of 'remembering'. And never does it occur in connection with pictures which refer back to day-experiences. We can therefore state that dream-images are not identical with memories.

In the same way that a dream-image avoids carrying even a slight quality of previous sense-impressions, so it also refrains from identifying itself with memories. Dreams are of a different stuff; they are neither the direct remnants of sense-impressions nor are they simply memory-pictures. What then is their real nature?

We may use a comparison which can perhaps help us to understand the peculiar existence of the fleeting impressions of dreams: with our eyes we behold the outer world, and with the assistance of other senses we accept the reality of these visual experiences. But there is another form of looking at the things outside. We can, for instance, place a mirror in front of any object, and instead of looking directly at the object, we perceive its mirror-picture. We are unable to connect this mirror-picture with other sense-experiences. It cannot be touched, tasted, and so on; we can just see it. Sometimes it is difficult to distinguish between such a picture and its object. At other times this distinction is quite obvious.

Do not all dreams have a similar character? Are they not mirror-images of something else? As soon as we realize this possibility, we at once grasp its reality. Yes, dreams are events which are seen in a mirror. My memories, my concepts, my ideas are mirrored and their images are my dream-impressions. I even mirror myself and appear as my own picture. We therefore said: 'The dream is not mine; it is rather the case that I, or a part of myself am also part of my dream.' The dream is outside myself, just as the mirror-image is not identical with its object. I behold my dream because I look into the mirror in which it appears.

The dream-mirror is not always as clear and never as inanimate as the mirror we use in daily life. The dream-mirror is full of living forces which have the ability to transform its pictures in a manifold way. This quality is fundamental for the whole life of dreams. It is the living power of the mirror itself that creates the immense variety of images.

This dream-mirror receives images from other spheres, too, not only from our own unconscious. The kingdom into which we enter after death can mirror its being in the dream-glass. The 'important' and the 'great' dreams are due to this mirroring. Rudolf Steiner said the following in one of his many references to dreams ([1915 June 22] 1981): 'Our common knowledge is the result of our daily life and its experiences. But our dreams are filled with inspirations which flow from the world of angels. And these angels again are inspired by beings of higher hierarchies.'

We carry a mirror with us through life. It is the mirror in which our dreams appear. At the same time, this very mirror can picture other events and beings. Rudolf Steiner therefore said in the same lecture:

> In point of fact, every one of us carries within himself a 'dreamer' who, so to speak, thinks and feels and wills with less intensity than we do in ordinary life. But this 'dreamer' is much wiser than we usually are. ... We do not recognize this 'dreamer' enough, but we do very many things of which we know very little, which the 'dreamer' in us guides and directs.

This 'dreamer in us' is part of our life and existence. It is neither identical with our body nor is it part of our soul. It is also not our unconscious or part of our emotional life. It is intimately connected with the living forces of life and metamorphosis in us. It is a stratum to which Rudolf Steiner refers as the structure of our formative forces — the builder of our physical organs the carrier of our thoughts and the bearer of our memories.

As long as our mind is awake and our senses are at work, the dreamer remains hidden. But as soon as we go to sleep and all senses stop functioning, the dreamer appears. Our limbs are relaxed, the sensory organs dumb, the central nervous system is at rest. And now the 'dreamer in us' takes possession of the resting brain and the spinal cord. Both lie enshrined in the hollow spaces of skull and spine. These two cavities are lined with the dura mater, a silvery, shining and densely woven layer of living tissue. This dura mater inside the skull is the spherical mirror for our dreams. Images from outside and memories from within appear, are mirrored, changed and transformed and thus become our dreams.

Our soul and spirit live around our body and are not enshrined in it during sleep. When a-dream, we look from outside on to the living images which are mirrored in the cavity of our skull and permeated and changed by the living forces of the 'dreamer'. The dream is not inside us; it appears by means of our body which at night is void of our soul. But the soul mirrors itself in the creative mirror of our skull. It sees and beholds its own mirror-image.

When we look into a mirror by day, we subconsciously remember our nightly experiences. We have a dim feeling that a similar process has produced our dreams during the night. In former times this knowledge was very common and the mirror was regarded as a magic tool. It was the symbol of the supersensory world of our dreams.

Synopsis

The mirror is a magic tool possessed by man since primeval times. The most beautiful mirrors from early civilizations are known to us. In Chaldea and Egypt, Greece and Rome mirrors were used. They did not only serve the pride and vanity of people. They helped man to recognize himself. For when he learned to look into the mirror, he began to behold his own countenance.

But he also learned to gaze through and beyond the mirror-picture of his countenance, and behind it the creative powers appeared which once had formed and moulded his face at the dawn of all evolution. This was the true meaning of the mirror! That man should, in the image of his own likeness, behold the image of God.

In the mysteries of Eleusis the pupils were told that once upon a time Dionysus looked into the mirror which Hephaestos, the lord of Hades, had forged for him. Dionysus was so deeply fascinated by his own image that he did not notice the Titans drawing near. They then took him and dismembered him into many parts. This is the story which was meant to warn the Orphic pupils not to succumb to their own mirror-image.

Paul, the Apostle, said: 'For now we see in a mirror dimly, but then face to face. Now I know in part; then I shall understand fully, even as I have been fully understood.' (1 Cor.13:12).

He refers to the narrowness of our consciousness. And he reminds us that a much wider knowledge, face to face, will be given to us after death. Just as we can now realize that our dreams are mirror-images and fleeting impressions, so shall we one day realize that our present life, though much more real, is narrow and little compared with the reality awaiting us after death.

Images now appear. The soul begins to speak of itself, to name itself, to describe its own being. The soul understands that different mirrors are used for different stages of consciousness and that these stages are steps which lead to an ever higher cognition.

Bibliography

Aeppli, Ernst. 1960. *Der Traum und seine Deutung*. Zürich.

Anders, G. 1956. *Die Antiquiertheit des Menschen*. München.

Bergson, Henri. 1919. *Materie und Gedächtnis*. Jena.

Brain, Russel. 1961. 'Consciousness and the Brain'. *Bewustseinsstörungen. Symposium*. Suttgart.

Brentano, Franz. 1889. *Vom Ursprung der sittlichen Erkenntnis*. Leipzig.

Burt, Cyril, 1962. 'The concept of consciousness'. *British Journal of Psychology*. 53:3.

Buytendijk, F. J. J. 1948. *Über den Schmerz*. Bern.

—, 1958. *Mensch und Tier*. Hamburg.

Castiglioni, A. 1946. *A History of Medicine*. New York.

Cohen, John. 1958. *Humanistic Psychology*. London.

Darwin, Charles. 1877. *The Expression of the Emotions in Man and Animal*. London.

Davies, Hallowell. 1962. 'The problem of consciousness'. *Symposium on Submarine and Space Medicine 1958*. New York.

Ewald, G. 1929. 'Über das optische Halluzinieren im Delirium und in verwandten Zuständen'. *Zeitschrift für Psychiatrie*. 71.

Flugel, J.C. 1945. *A Hundred Years of Psychology*. London.

Freud, Sigmund. 1933. *Vorlesungen zur Einführung in die Psychoanalyse*. Berlin.

Gebsattel, V.E. von 1954. *Prolegomena einer medizinischen Anthropologie*. Berlin.

Goodenough, F.L. 1945. *Developmental Psychology*. New York.

Gruhle, H.W. 1956. *Verstehende Psychologie*. Stuttgart.

Haensel, C. 1946. *Das Wesen der Gefühle*. Überlingen.

Hillman, James. 1960. *Emotion, a Comprehensive Phenomenology of Theories and their Meaning for Therapy*. London.

Hoche, A.E. 1927. *Das träumende Ich*. Jena.

Jacobi, Jolande. 1957. *Komplex, Archetypus, Symbol in der Psychologie C. G. Jungs*. Zürich.

James, William. 1892. *Textbook on Psychology*. London.

Jersild, A.T. 1954. 'Emotional development'. *A Manual of Child Psychology*. Ed. L. Carmichael. New York & London.

Jones, Ernest. 1953. *Sigmund Freud*. Vol. 1. London.

—, 1957. *Sigmund Freud*. Vol. 3. London.

Jung. C.G. 1962. *Erinnerungen, Träume, Gedanken*. Zurich & Stuttgart.

Kretschmer, E. 1929. *Körperbau und Charakter*. Berlin.

Leonhard, K. 1951. *Gesetze und Sinn des Träumens*. Stuttgart.

Lersch, Philipp. 1943. *Seele und Welt*. Leipzig.

Lewis, C.S. 1940. *The Problem of Pain*. London.

Lewis, Thomas. 1942. *Pain*. New York.

Loosli-Usteri, M. 1948. *Die Angst des Kindes*. Bern.

Lynd, H. Merell. 1958. *On Shame and the Search for Identity*. London.

Marquis, D.G., *see* Woodworth, R. S., & D. G. Marquis.

Martin, J. Purdon. 1949. 'Consciousness and its disturbances'. *Lancet*. 1:1.

McDougall, William. 1923. *An Outline of Psychology*. London.

McKellar, Peter. 1952. *A Textbook of Human Psychology*. London.

Mitchell, A. 1905. *About Dreaming, Laughing and Blushing*. Edinburgh & London.

Müller, L.R. 1948. *Über den Schlaf*. Berlin & München.

Plessner, H. 1950. *Lachen und Weinen*. Bern.

Portmann, A. 1953. *Das Tier als soziales Wesen*. Zürich.

Pötzl, O. 1917. 'Experimentell erregte Traumbilder in ihrer Beziehung zum direkten Sehen'. *Neurologie* 37:3/4.

Sheldon, W.H. 1942. *The Varieties of Temperament*. New York.

Steiner, Rudolf. [1894] 1964. *The Philosophy of Freedom*. London.

—, [1894] 1978. *Die Philosophie der Freiheit*. Dornach. GA 4.

—, [1907] 1979. *Die Theosophie der Rosenkreutzer*. Dornach. GA 99.

—, [1907] 1981. *Theosophy of the Rosicrucians*. London.

—, [1909] 1928. 'Die Temperamente im Lichte der Geisteswissenschaft'. *Die Menschenschule*. 2:2/3.

—, [1909] 1934. *Paths of Experience*. London.

—, [1909] 1971. *The Four Temperaments*. New York.

—, [1910] 1971. *The Wisdom of Man, of the Soul, and of the Spirit*. New York.

—, [1910] 1976. *The Christ Impulse and the Development of Ego Consciousness*. New York.

—, [1910] 1980. *Anthroposophie, Psychosophie, Pneumatosophie*. Dornach. GA 115.

—, [1910] 1982. *Der Christus-Impuls und die Entwickelung des Ich-Bewusstseins*. Dornach. GA 116.

—, [1913] 1928. *Secrets of the Threshold*. London & New York.

—, [1913] 1982. *Die Geheimnisse der Schwelle*. Dornach. GA 147.

—, [1915] 1981. *Menschenschicksale und Völkerschicksale*. Dornach. GA 157.

—, [1917] 1983. *Von Seelenrätseln*. Dornach. Steiner. GA 21.

—, [1918] 1985. *Erdensterben und Weltenleben*. Dornach. GA 181.

—, [1919] 1967. *Discussions with Teachers*. London.

—, [1919] 1977. *Erziehungskunst. Seminarbesprechungen und Lehrplanvorträge*. Dornach. GA 295.

—, [1920] 1935. *Colour*. London & New York.

—, [1920] 1980. *Das Wesen der Farben*. Dornach. GA 291.

—, [1920] 1985. *Geisteswissenschaft als Erkenntnis der Grundimpulse sozialer Gestaltung*. Dornach. GA 199.

—, [1924] 1979. *Heilpädagogischer Kursus*. Dornach. GA 317.

—, [1924] 1981a. *Anthroposophie. Eine Zusammenfassung*. Dornach. GA 234.

—, [1924] 1981b. *Curative Education*. London.

—, [1924] 1983. *Anthroposophy. An Introduction*. London.

Stern, William. 1928. *Psychologie der frühen Kindheit*. Leipzig.

Straus, Erwin, 1960. *Psychologie der menschlichen Welt*. Berlin.

Usteri, M. Loosli, see Loosli-Usteri, M.

Walsh, E.G. 1957. *Physiology of the Nervous System*. London.

Woodworth, R.S. & D.G. Marquis. 1952. *Psychology*. London.

Wright, Samson. 1952. *Applied Physiology*. London.

Zeylmans van Emmichoven. F.W. 1953. *Die menschliche Seele*. Basel.

Index

Aeppli, Ernst 145f, 148
Anders, G. 65
anger 57–60, 69
annoyance 58f
anxiety 46f, 50f
Aristotle 85
awakeness 117

Bergson 18, 43
Bergson, Henri 42
blush 66
Brain, Sir Russel 112
Brentano, Franz 28, 100
Burt, Cyril 109
Buytendijk, F.J.H. 44, 90

Castiglioni, A. 75
choleric 74, 86–88
Chuang Tzu 144
Cohen, John 10
consciousness 109–11, 120–22, 124–27

Darwin, Charles 55
Davies, Hallowell 116
desire 34f
discrimination 33f
dreams 132–50

ego 67
emotion 54f

Eros 35f
ethology 89
Ewald, G. 140

fear 46f, 61–63, 68f
feminine 35
Flugel, J.C. 67
Freud, Sigmund 18, 67, 135

Gebsattel, V.E. 46
Goethe, Johann W. von 30, 84, 87, 131
Goodenough, F.L. 72
Gruhle, H.W. 75, 85

Haensel, C. 62
hear 104
hearing 103
Heidegger, Martin 48
Heraclitus 25, 79
Hillman, James 79
Hippocrates 74, 85
Homer 58
Husserl, Edmund 28

id 67
intentionality 28f, 100, 102

Jackson, Hughlings 113
Jacobi, Jolande 123
James, William 55, 109–10, 112

Jersild, A.T. 63
Jones, Ernest 67, 135
Jung, C.G. 123, 145, 148

Kretschmer, E. 84f

laughing 18–20, 22
Leonhard, K. 138f, 142f
Lersch, Philipp 30
Lewis, C.S. 40f
Lewis, Sir Thomas 40
Loosli-Usteri, M. 48
Lynd, H. Merell 65, 67

Marquis, D.G. 54
Martin, Purdon 109, 113f
masculine 35
McDougall, William 10, 53–57, 134
McKellar, Peter 55, 58f, 72, 85
melancholic 74, 86–88
mind 11f, 16
Mitchell, A. 62, 64
mood 71–74, 79–81, 83, 89f
Müller, L.R. 143
music 98–100

pain 40f, 43, 46, 51
phlegmatic 74, 86f, 90
phobias 63
Plessner, H. 19, 21, 56, 60
Portmann, A. 89

Pötzl, O. 138
Psyche 35f

sanguine 74, 86, 88–90
Scheler, Max 28
Schuré, Eduard 27, 30
seeing 103f
senses 81f, 93, 95, 97, 99, 105
shame 61f, 64–66, 68f
Sheldon, W.H. 85
soul 12
sound 98–100
Steiner, Rudolf 20, 28f, 33, 42, 45, 49, 59, 67, 76, 85–87, 95, 101, 111, 121f, 125f, 138, 150f
Stern, William 47
Straus, E. 117–19
super-ego 67

temperament 74f, 77
temperaments 76, 84f
Titchener, Edward B. 59
transcendent 32f, 35
transcendent nature 30

Walsh, E.G. 44
Watson, John Broadus 109f
weeping 18–20, 22
Woodworth, R.S. 54

Zeylmans van Emmichoven, F.W. 25

The Karl König Archive series

Vol 1 Karl König: My Task
   Autobiography and Biographies

Vol 2 Karl König's Path into
   Anthroposophy
   Reflections from his Diaries

Vol 3 Ita Wegman and Karl König
   Letters and Documents

Vol 4 The Child with Special Needs
   *Letters and Essays on
   Curative Education*

Vol 5 Seeds for Social Renewal
   The Camphill Village Conferences

Vol 6 The Inner Journey Through the Year
   Soul Images and The Calendar of the Soul

Vol 7 The Calendar of the Soul
   A Commentary

Vol 8 Becoming Human: A Social Task
   The Threefold Social Order

Vol 9 Communities for Tomorrow

Vol 10 At the Threshold of the Modern Age
   Biographies Around the Year 1861

Vol 11 Brothers and Sisters
   The Order of Birth in the Family

Vol 12 Kaspar Hauser and Karl König

Vol 13 Animals
   An Imaginative Zoology

Vol 14 Social Farming
   Healing Humanity and the Earth

Vol 15 Nutrition from Earth and Cosmos

Vol 16 The Grail and the
   Development of Conscience
   St Paul and Parsifal

Vol 17 Plays for the Festivals of the Year

Vol 18 The Spirit of Camphill
   Birth of a Movement

Floris Books

For news on all our **latest books**,
and to receive **exclusive discounts**,
join our mailing list at:

florisbooks.co.uk

Plus subscribers get a FREE book
with every online order!

We will never pass your details to anyone else.